Dolce Far Niente:
Sweet Doing Nothing

Dolce Far Niente: Sweet Doing Nothing

A Journey through the Italian Countryside

A Travel Memoir

Paul L. Gentile

Ralph,
I hope you enjoy reading about our little Italian adventure. All the best,
Paul

iUniverse, Inc.

New York Lincoln Shanghai

Dolce Far Niente: Sweet Doing Nothing
A Journey through the Italian Countryside

iUniverse books may be ordered through booksellers or by contacting:

iUniverse
2021 Pine Lake Road, Suite 100
Lincoln, NE 68512
www.iuniverse.com
1-800-Authors (1-800-288-4677)

Because of the dynamic nature of the Internet, any Web addresses or links contained in this book may have changed since publication and may no longer be valid.

The views expressed in this work are solely those of the author and do not necessarily reflect the views of the publisher, and the publisher hereby disclaims any responsibility for them.

ISBN: 978-0-595-45423-5 (pbk)
ISBN: 978-0-595-69582-9 (cloth)
ISBN: 978-0-595-89736-0 (ebk)

Printed in the United States of America

For Joyce, my travel partner through life.

For Paul, Sandy, Brad, Susan, and Heather.

Contents

List of Photos

All photos were taken by the author. They are

Positano, Italy (front cover)

Cocullo, Italy

Pacentro, Italy

Gardens, Villa Vignamaggio

Florence from Piazzale Michelangelo

Castello D'Alboa, Radda

Venice

Palazzo Publico, Siena

Assisi from hotel window

Author, wife, and Italian relatives at Roseto degli Abruzzi

Villa Cimbrone, Ravello

Positano

Piazza 9 Aprile, Taormina, Sicily

Arch at end of Corso Umberto, Taormina

Author and wife at Café Quadri, St. Mark's Square, Venice

Door in village of Civitella, Tuscany

Acknowledgments

No author ever writes a book alone. This memoir is no exception. Because of all the wonderful people we met throughout Italy, our trip was an experience of a lifetime, filled with fondest memories. I am sincerely appreciative of my family in Italy for their unquestioning hospitality and affection, and for lovingly sharing stories of my father. I would like to extend a special thank-you to Nancy, a most gracious hostess, who took time to contact my relatives and arrange our visit. Thanks to Brad for the map of Italy and technical assistance with my photos; and to Suzanne Altman of impeccable grammar, who carefully proofread my manuscript, correcting this writer's spelling and punctuation with tact and encouragement.

I especially owe gratitude to Joyce, my guide and conscience, who read and reread every draft, cheerfully giving thoughtful suggestions and words of support. To her I am ever indebted.

Thanks to Famous Music LLC for permission to reprint lyrics to

Moon River
From the Paramount Picture BREAKFAST AT TIFFANY'S
Words by Johnny Mercer
Music by Henry Mancini
Copyright © 1961 (Renewed 1989) by Famous Music LLC
International Copyright Secured All Rights Reserved

"The world is a book and those who do not travel read only one page."

—St. Augustine

Introduction

I vividly remember the day I went over the edge—and toward my trip to Italy.

On the way home from work, I stopped at the grocery store, where the checkout clerk talked on her cell the entire time she rang me up. Never meeting my eyes or speaking to me, she dropped a pile of uncounted change in my hand without missing a word of her conversation. I wanted to smash that cell phone into the side of her head.

Part of my anger was a result of the frustration I was feeling over my current situation. Going to work was becoming a chore. After bypass surgery and a scare with a blood disorder, it was time to retire—this time for good. That meant no consulting, no excuses, and no guilt. I didn't feel sure about leaving, and I didn't feel good about staying. I hated all the comments like "You're too young to retire," "What will you do with all your free time?" and on and on. But I did it—I retired.

My wife, Joyce, also talked about retiring. She too was feeling the strain of our situation; on top of the demands of our jobs, we were feeling the squeeze of the sandwich generation, and she had been terribly worried about my health. All of our "free" time was so consumed with family obligations that we barely had the chance for a conversation.

Joyce felt guilty about retiring—and worried that she would find herself staring into a void after running on high for so long. The thought of leaving the workforce gave her a feeling of separation anxiety and a sense of loss. Retirement seemed like the end—an acknowledgment that life was over. I tried to give her a pep talk. But who was I to give advice? Just listening to all of those retirement comments had made me homicidal, so obviously, they got to me too.

So I suggested the one thing that always lifted our spirits: travel!

Joyce and I love to travel. We had even run our own travel agency for a while. We had crossed the United States and visited Mexico, Canada, Bermuda, and most countries in western Europe, always doing the planning and booking ourselves. We liked steering our own ship that way; it added adventure to our voyages and gave us a great sense of fulfillment.

This seemed like the perfect time for a trip. It would be a retirement celebration and, since it was the year of our fortieth wedding anniversary, a perfect gift to each other. We would go to Europe.

Perhaps you have had similar experiences. Maybe you are sick of cell phones, bad manners, and the general rush of American life. You might want to get away from it all for a while; take a vacation; go to Europe on your own. If so, then I have a story for you that will offer details to help you plan your own trip to Italy. In addition, I'll talk of doing ancestry research and meeting family members. I'll also talk about attending a cooking school in Tuscany and will give you a few recipes. I hope that my anecdotes offer insight, humor, and a little practical know-how when it comes to spending four weeks in a beautiful country.

Planning the Trip

Have you ever thought about traveling to Europe but felt it was too big an undertaking to arrange on your own? If you don't like group tours, it's easy to put off the planning—and your dream trip—indefinitely. Yet independent travel is a wonderful, enriching, and freeing experience … and something anyone can do. It doesn't take training or special background, just desire and planning. You start with four Ws and an H: who, what, where, when, and how.

Joyce and I decided to spend a month in Italy, leaving when school started in the fall to get the feeling of being retired (we had both been in the field of education.). This allowed us six months for the planning. After all, anticipation and planning are part of the fun.

During our past travels, we had avoided group tours, which packed too much into a small time frame. If you've ever participated in such a tour, you know the drill: navigating a whirlwind of three or four countries; seeing every sight mentioned in the tour books via trains, massive tour buses, and miles of walking; and eating pre-determined meals with the same big group of people over and over again. Despite our desire to avoid this circus, we always did want to see everything and would still manage to pack too much into a short period of time. We'd return home flushed with excitement, but exhausted and overstimulated.

This time would be different. We would spend a month just in Italy. We would avoid Rome and Florence and any of the other highly traveled tourist haunts. We had been there and done that. This time, we would spend a whole month in the country, getting a feel for the people and the lifestyle. For years, we'd dreamed of renting a place in Europe and exploring outward in brief day trips. That's what we would do. The idea was to immerse ourselves in the culture, maybe even attend one of those popular cooking schools. And I'd set aside some time to research my family tree.

My father was born in the Italian province of Abruzzo, and his father lived with us when I was a child, but neither of them talked much about their birthplace. When I was twelve, my grandfather retired from the steel mill and returned to Italy, rejoining my dad's two sisters. My grandfather had come to America alone as a young, married man to make money for the homestead, making return trips to see his wife and children. After his wife died at the age of thirty-four, he stopped going back to Italy. As each son was old enough to work in the steel mill, they came to the United States, but the girls stayed in Italy. My aunts had since died, but I still had two cousins. I didn't know anything about them or where they lived. At best, I hoped to research our family records in the village church; at the very least, I wanted to learn the names of my great-grandparents.

Other than the rare holiday telephone call while I was growing up, we had no contact with family members in Italy. My father used to talk of the beautiful mountains and streams where he walked as a young boy, but he left at fifteen, so we had no stories of contemporary Italy. After my grandfather died, all communication ended. My relatives in Italy seemed an abstraction, and I wanted to know more about them. This trip might offer my only chance to connect with my paternal ancestry.

I plunged into the research. We would use our frequent-flyer miles for the flight, get a rental car for the month, and stay off the beaten path. I used the Internet to research Italian cooking schools, rental cars, and companies that rented villas (some even offered house exchanges). I also located sites for genealogical research.

Our excitement grew as our plans took shape. We'd fly into Rome, get the car at the airport, and head for our rental villa, our home base for the month. I wanted to spend a few days in my ancestral village and some time at the Amalfi Coast. Several companies provided fascinating cooking classes, but which one should we take?

I had forgotten how frustrating Internet research could be. I would get stuck in a seemingly blind alley, jam the keyboard, and get into hopeless positions that no Back button could untangle. Since I couldn't yell out for my secretary to save me anymore, I would shut down improperly and get scolded by the machine after it restarted. I have a real love/hate relationship with my computer.

When I had gotten as far as I could online, I contemplated my next step. What to do? Go to the bookstore and buy a few hundred dollars' worth of travel books and magazines on Italy? Buy learning materials to familiarize myself with the native language? In Europe, the language barrier is nearly nonexistent in the major cities and at major tourist sites, because nearly everyone speaks English to some degree. However, I wanted to learn Italian to communicate in smaller villages, where possibly no one spoke English and, hopefully, converse with my relatives.

I had never learned Italian as a child; my grandfather insisted on speaking English. In those days, immigrants were concerned about assimilating into the American culture. Some didn't want people to know their origins because of the negative attitude toward Italy after the Second World War. Maybe that's why my family did not speak Italian—except among their friends and when they didn't want us to know what they were saying. Now I really regretted my youthful disinterest. I wanted to know and speak the language.

Community colleges offer short language courses designed to give you enough rudimentary knowledge to get by on a trip. Even though many Italians speak English, they are pleased when you try to speak their language and will generally reward your enthusiasm with great patience. Such communication offers a unique way to get to know them. Unsuccessful at registering for an Italian course, I bought a set of CDs to learn Italian the "easy" way—in the car. The relatively inexpensive system seemed simple: just pop a disc in the player while driving, and wham, you've learned a new language … or so I thought. But I listened diligently to the discs up to the day of our departure—when alone in the car, that is.

Our home office was filled with books, brochures, and maps—not to mention all the old stuff I had dug up from previous European trips. Up to this time, I had done most of the research. But if you are traveling with a partner, you really have to plan together. And you can't do it on the run. You need to dedicate the time and work at it. As I was charging ahead, Joyce was feeling left out of the planning.

So it was agreed: on the upcoming Saturday, we would grab all these materials and a bottle of wine, sit outside on the deck, and map the trip. It would be fun doing this together.

On Saturday, I gathered up all the work I had done, Joyce got the wine and a snack, and we proceeded to the deck to start planning. To determine our itinerary, we each would list our desired destinations, then combine the lists to eliminate duplication.

Joyce and I wrote furiously, then read our choices to each other. We had agreed we wanted to spend time on the Amalfi Coast, most likely Positano or Sorrento, and Joyce wanted to see Capri. I had suggested we attend a cooking school in Tuscany. She loved the idea. I also wanted to research my family tree in Abruzzo. That was fine with her too. This was going great.

Then Joyce interrupted. She would like to go to her ancestral villages, which were in France. I explained that we didn't have enough time to go to France. I reminded her about our decision not to pack too much into our trips. We'd stick to Italy this time and visit France exclusively next time.

Joyce agreed, adding that she wanted to go to Padua and Saint Anthony's Basilica. For two years, we'd made the thirteen-week novena to Saint Anthony at a lovely little chapel dedicated to him in the Troy Hill section of Pittsburgh. Troy Hill is an old neighborhood settled by Germans in the early nineteenth century. In the neighborhood's early days, the pastor of their Catholic church, an Austrian from a wealthy family, purchased religious icons and relics from Europe and built a chapel to house them. Dedicated to Saint Anthony of Padua, the chapel has become second only to Rome for the number of icons and relics in its collection.

The Saint Anthony Chapel is a beautiful hidden jewel in Pittsburgh, and the novena ceremonies are most moving. Having gotten a local glimpse of that beauty and piety, we both wanted to experience Padua and the Basilica where Saint Anthony is actually buried.

Also, Joyce wanted to visit her cousins in Austria and see Sicily. Again, I reminded her about spreading ourselves too thin all over Europe. "Do you know how far it is from Tuscany to Padua to Austria to Sicily?" I asked.

She glared at me. "You don't have to bite my head off. This is supposed to be enjoyable. Do you always have to do everything your way?"

We took a break to relieve the tension. I do tend to tackle too much on my own and am a bit obsessive when it comes to planning trips. I thought about it and decided I had to relax and truly work with Joyce in the spirit of partnership. We went back to work and came up with our plan.

First, we'd get our plane tickets, locking in our departure and return dates. We were concerned about US Airways' recent financial problems and thought we'd better use our frequent-flyer miles soon. Besides, it would be great to fly that distance first class. After a half hour on the phone with US Airways, I had booked our seats. We would fly first class from Pittsburgh to Frankfurt, then on Lufthansa from Frankfurt to Florence. Our planned departure and return dates had to be changed, and we would have to return via Venice to Frankfurt to Pittsburgh. But at least we were going first class. A word to the wise: when using frequent-flier miles, book far in advance, since those seats are limited and fill quickly.

Selecting a cooking school was our next step—and yet another advantage of planning our own trip. We chose a class that combined our two loves: "Walking and Cooking in Tuscany." The class ran six days and took place on a thousand-acre working farm converted into a resort (*fattoria*). There were only two days of cooking classes, but wine and olive-oil tastings were included. Many such programs were tightly organized, with guides and bus tours. This one was open and independent.

For some, the next step would be booking accommodations, but we like to get our rooms as we travel, so we can see them before making a commitment. Also, booking on the fly grants the flexibility to change itineraries and negotiate rates. This is not the case with train tickets or rental cars; it is important to take care of your transportation needs while still in America. Prior to embarking on a previous trip, we had bought a Eurail pass, good for unlimited use for a month on any train in any western European country. Those deals and special rates are only available if booked in advance—and from the United States. For this trip, Auto

Europe had the best deals. We would get the car in Florence and return it twenty-eight days later in Venice. With that reservation made, it was time to map out the rest of the trip.

A priority for Joyce was to be in Padua on a Tuesday—a special day for visits to St. Anthony's tomb. Another priority was a stop in Deruta to buy pottery, and she still wanted to see Sicily. We decided to visit the north first, heading south as the weather cooled. That way, we'd enjoy maximum time in good weather and some beach time. We would book the cooking school first, since it would be close to Florence. The free time in the cooking-school schedule would allow us to squeeze in a visit to Arezzo, only twenty kilometers away. If there was enough time, we would drive to Montalcino and Montipulciano to sample their great wines.

After cooking school, we would head for Venice to be in Padua on a Tuesday, then work our way south: San Gimignano and Volterra to see the Etruscan ruins and artifacts; Siena, Cortona, and Deruta for pottery; Assisi for St. Francis's hermitage; Gubio, Spoleto, and Orvieto in Umbria; my ancestral home in Abruzzo; Positano on the Amalfi Coast; Capri; and then Sicily. We chose Taormina as our Sicily stop, because it was a beachside resort. This seemed like a busy itinerary, but it included nice chunks of time along the way to get some rest. Spread over a month, this itinerary didn't seem bad—at least not in theory.

But then we would have to drive all the way back to Venice to catch our flight home. That could be a chore. Joyce felt we should turn the car in at Taormina and take the train to Venice as a relaxing and romantic end to our trip. I thought we should keep the car and drive back in two days. After all, we take such road trips all the time in America. Americans need to have their cars, no matter where they go. That was it, then: the entire trip would be by car.

Since we'd decided to cover the whole boot of Italy, the idea of a home base at a villa was out. Maybe we could book a villa for a week at Positano. My research showed villas were not very economical. In addition to the weekly rent, tenants paid extra charges for utilities and parking. Then we would have to buy groceries and do our own cooking. While excited about our cooking class, we didn't want to spend a lot of time in Positano shopping for groceries. We decided to pull out all stops and splurge for a nice hotel room instead.

I worked on the computer and pored over my guidebooks with a vengeance, booking hotels, researching family, and stockpiling knowledge of all the cultural and artistic sights to include as we crossed Italy. I found my most reliable and trusted source to be Frommer's guides. Frommer's *Tuscany and Umbria* and Frommer's *Italy from $70 a Day* (now $90 a day) were excellent for directions, lodging and dining suggestions, and town or village maps. Karen Brown's Guides were excellent sources for unique and charming places to stay. Baedeker's *Italy* was an excellent resource for sightseeing in any location, including some of the out-of-the-way places we wanted to visit. I decided to book hotels in Venice, Positano, Assisi, and Taormina, where lodging might be hard to get at the last minute. These hotels also would be the most expensive, so I wanted to take advantage of Internet specials. For flexibility, I would book the other places as we arrived.

Work on the trip was proceeding well. Friends and family asked about our plans. Most matched our high enthusiasm, except for the friend who pleaded with me not to go because of the troubling world situation. "I don't want to see you on the evening news with a sack over your head." I thanked him for the vivid imagery and continued planning.

I found the name of an English-speaking woman named Nancy who lived in Bugnara, the hometown of my father. I got her phone number from her cousin who lived near us and gave her a call. Nancy had lived in the United States for a few years but hadn't cared much for it, so she had moved back to Italy with her mother and brother several years ago. During our conversation, I discovered she was related to my godfather, my father's childhood friend who had lived near us when I was growing up.

Nancy and I talked for almost an hour. She would be happy to spend a day or two with us and act as our interpreter. Plus, she lived next to our family home and knew my cousin, Tilde. Although Tilde taught math near Rome, which was an hour and a half away, Nancy would ask her to travel to Bugnara to meet us. I considered this a wonderful prospect. I was far enough along on our itinerary to provide the date we would arrive in Sulmona, the nearest town to Bugnara with a hotel. I said I would call when we arrived and thanked her for agreeing to help us.

Plans for the trip were developing smoothly … but then it started.

As our departure date neared, the papers were filled with bad news about US Airways. They would stop the flights from Pittsburgh to Frankfurt, presumably two weeks after our return home. If US Airways did not get concessions from the unions, they might ground their planes. Listening to a radio show featuring our county administrator, Joyce was so distraught that she called on her cell phone and told him of our dilemma. He was in negotiations with US Airways regarding the airline's fate in Pittsburgh and would surely be able to tell her something to put our minds at ease. He was polite but could tell her nothing definite. The guy had to know what was going on, yet he couldn't give us answers.

Other flights to Italy were expensive and filling fast, due to the closeness to our departure date. Then US Airways announced they would soon make a decision on whether to file for Chapter 11 or Chapter 13. The former would mean they could keep flying; the latter would ground their planes. This decision would be made three days before we were to leave.

I cycled between frustration, anger, and despair. What if they did ground the planes three days before we were to leave? All these plans would be for nothing, and I would have to fight to recover thousands of dollars. What if they grounded the planes after we landed in Italy? Would other airlines honor our tickets for home? This was being discussed in the media and the answer was yes—unless those tickets had been acquired with frequent-flyer miles. Great! I had decided to use my frequent-flyer miles at a time when they could become worthless. What could I do? I bought a travel insurance policy for our cooking school, the largest single expenditure at that point. Also, I vowed to stop reading the news on US Airways. Whatever would be would be.

At the same time, the news revealed growing tensions in the East, the problems in Iraq, and negative reactions to Americans in Europe. And the value of the dollar was dropping. Would we be able to get there, and what would we face when we did? Would we be the only Americans foolish enough to travel abroad this fall? Would everyone hate us? We bought hiking sandals instead of tennis shoes, so we wouldn't look so much like American tourists. The vision my friend had painted of us with bags over our heads haunted my dreams. People were eager to give us bad news and offer precautionary advice. Should I stop reading and watching the news altogether? I chose to continue planning and hope for the best.

Of real concern was how our mothers would manage without us for a whole month. In addition to guilt about retiring, concern about the world situation, and frustration with US Airways, we felt worry for the parents who had come to rely so heavily on our help. Our anxiety level was very high. We were totally stressed.

I typed a detailed itinerary, including the names and phone numbers of places we had booked. We gave these to our children, along with schedules outlining their responsibilities in taking care of their grandmothers. We promised to e-mail them from cybercafés with updates on additional accommodations we'd arranged. Plans for lawn care, mail and paper delivery, and every possible disaster scenario were set in place. Three days before our departure, US Airways announced they would file for Chapter 11. Their planes would continue to fly.

Finally, it was time to pack. We prided ourselves on being light packers. Joyce had a special trick: she followed a color scheme. Every garment she packed was black, white, or some pattern of the two, allowing an interchangeability that resulted in many different outfits. Then, using colorful scarves and accessories, she could dress an outfit up or down to suit most situations. We both would wear blazers on the plane to conserve valuable suitcase space. I packed polo shirts and only four pairs of underwear and socks—the kind that can be washed in a bathroom sink and hung to dry overnight. We stored laundry detergent in a small plastic container. We traveled light, yet stayed prepared for any occasion, from casual to dressy.

On a previous trip to Europe, we had gotten everything into two carry-ons. Friends could not believe it. With only one carry-on each, we hadn't had to wait for baggage check-ins or claims—or worse, haggle over lost luggage. But this time, our concern was packing for both hot and cold weather. We might have snow as early as October in the northern mountains, yet be able to swim in Sicily. We decided on one regular suitcase and two carry-ons. Joyce would put all her things in the suitcase; I would put mine in a carry-on. Since we had to check her suitcase, we would check mine too. Then we would use the second carry-on for her cosmetics, my shaving things, medicines, and a change of underwear in case the checked luggage was lost.

Since flight security has tightened, many items are no longer permitted as carry-on. Check with your carrier for regulations. As a traveler, you must always be prepared for change.

We're Off

The day finally came when we were taken to the airport by our daughter, Heather. Joyce wanted to make sure we got there early enough to enjoy time in the first-class lounge. We sailed through an unhassled international, first-class check-in and headed for the first-class lounge—and our first bit of relaxation in more than a month. I sipped on my complimentary drink and watched people talking on phones, working on their computers, reading the complimentary paper, and watching the plasma TV. Surveying my surroundings I wondered what the coach people were doing. Still standing in that horrendous line at coach check-in? Or perhaps buying a Big Mac to eat while sitting in those awful chairs at the gate? I returned my attention to my drink and snacks.

A half hour before boarding time, we casually strolled to our gate, not wanting to miss the early call for first-class boarding and the complimentary preflight drink. But the plane was delayed—first a half hour, then another hour … and finally, four hours. I had to have our Frankfurt connection changed. Customer-service representatives told me there were two more flights from Frankfurt to Florence. The problem was that the first of the two flights, which was scheduled to leave at 12:30 PM, was booked. The agent would put us on standby for that flight and confirm us on the second flight, which was scheduled for a 4:30 PM departure and had room.

The waiting area at the gate had become crowded and the mood agitated. People were looking out the window at the activity around our plane and starting to speculate. Rumors were being circulated, tempers were rising. Over the public-address system, a voice announced the flight was being delayed because the cappuccino maker was malfunctioning. People howled in disbelief and came forth with several uncharitable suggestions for what could be done with the cappuccino maker. The relaxing effects of the first-class lounge had totally evaporated. Near us, someone confirmed that the cappuccino maker had actually created a serious problem; it was giving off fumes that made a flight attendant sick, and a replacement attendant had to be found. We had seen a flight attendant taken away by ambulance. That made sense.

Finally, we boarded the plane, settling into the second row of first class. We were given complimentary mimosas, pillows, blankets, toilet kits, and menus for dinner. The flight attendant hung up my jacket. I could feel the blood slowing down in my veins; vacation had officially begun. Clinking our mimosa glasses together, Joyce and I toasted the beginning of a wonderful adventure. After enjoying our gourmet meal and sipping an after-dinner drink, we put on headsets and tuned into some relaxing music. "Moon River," our dating and wedding song, was playing. We held hands and toasted again. I drifted off to sleep feeling very fortunate.

It was ten Monday morning as we made our descent to the Frankfurt airport. Before we landed, we passed over the Rhine and its lush, verdant hills; several barges navigating this marvelous river; an occasional castle; and then a huge atomic power plant; some industry; and the unremarkable skyline of Frankfurt. It was a jolt to leave the warm security created by our flight attendants and converge into the hustle of the airport and our first sense of culture shock on the trip so far. Amid the chaos of a different language and flight charts flipping with changing information, we tried to figure out where we were and where to go. It was comforting to find the gate for our flight to Florence, but we also discovered that not only was the 12:30 PM flight overbooked, but in Pittsburgh they had only booked one of us on the 4:30 PM flight—the last one for the day, that was also now full. What were we to do?

I suggested that if one of us could get on the twelve-thirty flight, the other could take the confirmed seat on the four-thirty flight, and we could meet at the Florence airport. "No way," said Joyce. "I'm not going to fly without you or be separated from you in a strange country where I don't know the language. We go together, or we both stay."

"Okay," I said. "If we don't get on the twelve-thirty flight, we'll look into taking a train from here to Florence."

"Do you think we could?"

"Sure, why not?" Silence. We both knew that wasn't going to work. We had no idea how to get to the train station, whether there would be a train to Florence, what it would cost, or how long it would take. Even if such a train existed, it might be an overnighter or not leaving until tomorrow, making us too late to pick up our rental car. The cooking school started the next day.

They were boarding the twelve-thirty flight. We have become experts at spotting other standby passengers, and there were a bunch. They started calling people to the desk. We knew each name being called was a person taking a seat that should be ours; we didn't like them. Have you ever had the experience of waiting to be called as others are sauntering up to get their tickets? Hearts race, palms sweat, and stomachs tighten.

Then they called our names. Unbelievable—we were getting on! They explained apologetically that there was only one seat left in coach and one in first class, so we could not sit together. Were they serious? Did we care? We were getting on. I magnanimously gave the first-class seat to Joyce, then sat in the very last seat of the plane next to a very large man who didn't talk, but loudly enjoyed the ham and cheese sandwich he was given. The flight attendant apologized; there was only a plain cheese sandwich left for me. I wasn't complaining; U.S. flights didn't always give so much as a bag of peanuts and charged ridiculous prices for a terrible sandwich. Meanwhile, Joyce was served a full meal on china. She sat next to a woman from Sonoma County, California, who owned a winery. They talked the whole trip, exchanged e-mail addresses, and planned to meet whenever we took a trip to California.

This plane was smaller and slower than our transatlantic plane, so it flew lower. I watched the scenery the entire way. Crossing over the Alps, I saw a familiar wishbone-shaped lake and knew it was Lake Como. We were crossing into Italy. I could see the crowning jewel of the lake, nestled at the point where you would break the wishbone for good luck: Bellagio, where Joyce and I had celebrated our thirtieth anniversary. Warm, wonderful memories came coursing back. Others looking out the window may have seen just another lake, but I saw a wonderful time of my life full of exquisite beauty and calm. We had been ten years younger, still planning and dreaming, absorbing all the new experiences with joy and excitement. The site of Bellagio, while filling me with nostalgia, suddenly gave me that jolt of energy that comes with expectation. We could be light and carefree again. Forget all that was waiting for us back home. We were here again; we could enjoy the moment and drink in the experience.

As we descended toward the Florence airport, I could see the changing hills, cypress-lined drives leading to ocher-colored stucco villas, and that picture-perfect countryside that was unmistakably Tuscany; then the industrial development along the Arno River, and in the distance, Brunelleschi's magnificent dome. At last, we were here. Upon landing, I joined Joyce and her seatmate, and we went to baggage claim. All the baggage streamed in, including the smaller carry-on style suitcase that we had checked ... and then nothing. Where was Joyce's bag? All the luggage was out; all but three of us had left the area. Our trio had to go to Lost and Found to file a claim.

Joyce had packed everything for the entire trip in that bag. Often, we'd share bags and pack by category. This time, we had decided I would have mine, and she would have hers. Why had we done that? They casually told us that if we filed a claim, our luggage would most likely be found and delivered to us within a week. A week! Without a change of clothes for Joyce?

We filed a claim giving the address of the cooking school and left the airport. Taxis lined up out front to whisk takers to the historic center of the city, which was three miles away, for twenty euros. A few yards beyond was a kiosk for the bus. For just four euros each, and no tip, the bus would let us off right across the street from the train station. There we could get a room for the night through the travel service. The bus ride was filled with silence. Joyce, I'm certain, was upset about her suitcase, and I was feeling guilty that it wasn't mine.

Arrival, Confusion, and Culture Shock

Florence is a unique city and a required stop for anyone going to Italy. As the seat of the Renaissance, it houses some of the most important art and history in the world, but it's more than that. Florence is the New York City of Italy—all the excitement, all the exasperation. We love New York. We enjoyed Florence for the same reasons: the city is always on the go, with traffic jams, honking horns, and people in a hurry. Street vendors, street artists, and street people crammed into narrow alleyways with two-foot-wide sidewalks or none at all, creating an overload of sight, sound, and smell. Elegant residents hurried by, mixed with loads of tourists and tour groups, their leaders jabbing the air with umbrellas or flags. Delivery trucks sped and honked, Vespas whizzed, and pickpockets slunk along. All are part of an integral package that you'll either love or hate. We loved it.

We arrived at the bus terminal, and then walked to the train station directly across the way. We aimed for the train boarding platforms in the back, where a tourist information office will give hotel information and book rooms for a five-euro fee. Like everything in Florence, it was packed.

Eventually, we chose a room at the three-star Hotel Goldoni on Borgo Ognissanti, a street lined with antique shops that runs through the heart of the historic district. The cost was 120 Euros, plus the five-euro fee—a little high for an on-the-road stay. But a successful escape from jet lag demands a good night's sleep. The hotel was two flights up from the street in a building that had once been a palazzo, although it had been a hotel since 1770—when, as the owners proudly advertised, Mozart spent some time there.

The hotel was air-conditioned, which we were glad of, because Florence was smoldering and humid. Our room had twelve-foot ceilings; marble floors; huge, shuttered, double-glazed windows, which kept out the street noise; and an adequate bath. It was spotlessly clean.

The historic district is very compact and walkable. As we were walking to the hotel, it occurred to me what might have happened to Joyce's bag. When the agent in Pittsburgh booked only one of us on the four-thirty flight from Frankfurt, she probably had one of the bags ticketed for that flight, and therefore, Joyce's bag would be on the four-thirty flight. We couldn't really enjoy this trip until that bag was recovered, so after we checked into the hotel and dropped off my bags, we immediately left for the bus terminal to get another bus back to the airport in an effort to retrieve Joyce's suitcase.

I noticed on our original ride that the bus had dropped off the departing crowd at the terminal and then waited fifteen minutes for the arriving people before leaving. The airport was small, and people leaving the baggage claim only had to exit from an electronic door to the outside walk. I didn't want to waste time going through security, so as people came out of the electronic door from baggage claim, I grabbed Joyce's hand, and we scurried in through the door. The flight had landed, and the bags were already on the conveyor. We spotted Joyce's bag. I grabbed it, ready to run out. Then I realized we should cancel the lost claim. When I told the woman at the desk that we had found the bag and she could cancel the claim, she asked how we had gotten into the area. I told her the truth and got a scolding for entering through the exit. She took us to a guard to report that we had breached security. The guard listened to her, looked at us, shrugged, and let us go. We were out of the terminal in time to get back on the same bus that had brought us.

Back at the hotel and feeling smugly successful, Joyce and I happily changed clothes and headed out for the evening. As we walked hand in hand through the historic neighborhoods, we gradually relaxed. We were in Italy! Walking past the tony shops of Via del Parione and Via Porta Rossa into Piazza della Signoria, between the towering copy of Michelangelo's *David* and the massive Fountain of Neptune, we found ourselves in the middle of *passeggiata*, the daily Italian activity where everyone goes out onto the streets and into the squares before dinner to walk, gossip, see, and be seen.

The piazza was filled with crowds walking in every direction among street performers and artists. Everyone was out strolling, window shopping, checking the restaurants for the evening meal, or eating gelato. Affluent and beautifully dressed locals, tourists in jeans and tennis shoes, street people—everyone under the cloudless sky was enjoying the delectable smells wafting from bakeries, pizzerias, and restaurants. Enchanted, Joyce and I gazed at this magnified mosaic of life in an Italian city. We decided to eat at Trattoria Marione on Via della Spada. This delightful little place offered seating in a cellar with vaulted brick ceiling. There seemed to be a lot of locals, which is always a good sign.

Before going any further, perhaps I should describe Italian eating habits, since the preparing and eating of food is a primary function of life in Italy. Have you heard the saying "There are people who eat to live and those who live to eat"? For the Italians, eating is living, and living is eating. It is more than a bodily function; it is an anchor to their culture, a key social activity. During my childhood, every important or unimportant event was celebrated around the dining-room table, and every meal was a social event filled with unhurried conversation and companionship.

The Italians are not big breakfast eaters. A usual Italian breakfast in the city may consist of a cappuccino quickly downed at a stand-up roadside bar on the way to work. Until recently, if a hotel included breakfast with the room, it was a basket of rolls (probably left over from dinner the night before) and some coffee with steamed milk. These breakfasts recently have become more diverse, probably in concession to the heavy influx of American and German travelers (who seem to be the heartiest breakfast eaters). Even so, you won't find fried eggs and bacon at an Italian breakfast. However, the other two meals of the day are elaborate productions.

Restaurants serve lunch from noon to three in the afternoon, and most businesses close for the occasion. The restaurants then close until seven in the evening, when they reopen to serve dinner into the late hours of the night. Seven is actually the respectable time to take part in the *passeggiata*, with dinner following around nine or so.

Both lunch and dinner consist of several courses. The meal will start with an antipasto, the Italian equivalent of an appetizer, and then proceed to the *primo piatto*, or first course, which is usually a pasta dish of some sort or soup. *Secondo piatto*, the second course, is usually seafood or meat. This may be accompanied by or followed by a salad of just greens, and then may end with a *dolce*, or a sweet—very often, fruit and cheese. The diner may choose to skip courses, but usually will eat the entire meal at least once a day.

At Trattoria Marione, we started with a bottle of Geografico Chianti Classico 2002; when in Tuscany, you must drink Tuscan wine. We then had a mixed-green salad and antipasto Nisto Toscana—a delightful mix of salamis, capacollo, and prosciutto. Next, Joyce chose a risotto from the *primo* section of the menu, and I had ossobucco alla Fiorentine, a melt-in-your-mouth journey of delight from the *secondo* section. Too stuffed for dessert, we paid our bill of thirty-three euros, which included the customary cover charge for sitting at a table, and the tip. An Asian couple next to us, obviously new to Italian dining, sat puzzling over the cover charge and tip. Judging from their looks of dismay, they were not getting a satisfactory—although quite detailed and dramatic—explanation from the waiter.

With full stomachs and a feeling of calm, we walked back to our hotel. The streets of Florence at night hold a bit of mystery; they are busy, but they are also dark and narrow. As in any city, it is best to enjoy the moment with your eyes and ears open. Back in our room, we slept like stones, then awoke refreshed and ready for our adventure. Breakfast was in a beautiful room—probably once the grand salon of the palazzo. Marble floors and a marble fireplace, a crystal chandelier, and tall open windows that let in the crisp morning air welcomed us to the continental breakfast of fruits, juices, croissants, and assorted breads and cakes, all complemented by cappuccinos.

After breakfast, we walked to the Ponte Vecchio (Old Bridge). This often-photographed, fourteenth-century bridge is lined with shops and is so beautiful that even Hitler couldn't bring himself to destroy it. Thus, it is the sole survivor of the dictator's bombs. Joyce browsed the jewelry stores and found them too pricey to buy from. We continued on to the carnival atmosphere of the Piazza del Duomo, with its maddening crush of tourists and student groups all vying for space with the street artists and vendors. I noticed an interesting opera being played out between the police and the Algerian street vendors selling designer knockoffs. Apparently, these folks were illegal, or selling without a permit. These vendors would open wooden suitcases and set them on stands, or spread their wares out on the ground. When a police officer would appear as if on cue, casually strolling down the street, these vendors would close their cases and act as if they were walking away. As soon as the officer passed, they would open their cases and continue bargaining with the person they had been dealing with before the interruption. Obviously, the police were as concerned about this little bit of illegal activity as the airport guard had been about our breaching security.

Ruling over this madness were Brunelleschi's magnificent red-tiled dome; Giotto's stately bell tower, banded in the same green, pink, and white marble as the church and baptistery; and Ghilberti's masterful bronze Baptistery doors. These three structures spanning three centuries are reason enough to visit Florence. On our previous visit, we had gone to the Academia to see the original Michelangelo's *David*, which had been moved from the Piazza della Signoria into the Academia to preserve it from deterioration by the elements. We also hit every church and the Medici chapels but were unable to go through the Uffizi, a must-see for the art enthusiast. That magnificent sixteenth-century palazzo-turned-museum houses the largest collection of Renaissance art in the world.

Sadly, we found ourselves once again in Florence on a Monday, when most of the museums are closed. So we decided to visit the Palazzo Medici-Riccardi, built in1444 for Cosimo de'Medici il Vecchio. It served as a prototype for the later Florentine Palazzi, and housed within its walls is the oldest chapel to survive from a private Florentine Palazzo. The fifteenth-century Chapel of the Magi's walls are covered with vivid and richly colored frescoes by Gozzoli, depicting the journey of the magi to see the Christ child.

Back outside were streets filled with booths where artisans sold jewelry, clothing, and leather goods at bargain prices. The buyer must check the quality of work, but it is possible to negotiate some real bargains. We didn't shop this time, however; we just had enough time to get back to our hotel, check out, and walk a few blocks to the Auto Europe office to get our rental car before they closed for the customary three-hour lunch.

The line at the rental agency spilled out into the street. After we waited for nearly an hour, lunchtime arrived. Mercifully, the office remained open, and we were given our Fiat Punta and directions for getting out of the city. While in line, I watched each person, couple, or family emerge from the building as an attendant pulled up to the curb with a wide array of cars, some sleeker than others. We had been going for the best deal, so I wasn't surprised when we walked out onto the street to find a gray tennis shoe on wheels. We jammed our three suitcases into the envelope-sized trunk and got in. I quickly familiarized myself with the interior, amazed that we had air-conditioning. The rest of the car was more typically European: spartan with a manual shift. After a quick look at our directions out of the city, we were on our way. I wanted to take the Chianti Road to the Fattoria Montelucci, where we would enjoy our week in cooking school. Chianti would be more picturesque than the Autostrada, Italy's version of a toll expressway, and we could stop at a few wineries along the way.

We promptly got lost trying to leave the city. I was on the southern side of the Arno, as I was supposed to be, but none of the street names matched our directions. I pulled to the side of the road and consulted the sketchy map provided by the rental agency. I also checked the Mapquest directions that I had printed before leaving home. Even though I had made all right turns at the designated intersections, which should have taken me across the Arno to the southeastern side of the city, we were now on the southwestern side. But by getting lost, we found one of those unexpected gems that make travel memorable.

I asked a man walking by how to get to SS222—which was the Chianti Road —and he gave me directions. Now, I was conversing in my best "learn Italian in your car" Italian, so to this day, I'm not sure if the roads we took were the roads he told us to take, but we found ourselves in the Oltrarno neighborhood. This is a combination working class-Bohemian neighborhood of narrow, confusingly winding streets and alleyways loaded with artisan's shops, cafés, and apartments. Driving around Piazza Santo Spirito, we passed the Pitti Palace and found ourselves in the baroque fantasy world of the Boboli Gardens, Florence's most beautiful Renaissance garden, worth a whole day in itself. We started to climb the winding road to Via Belvedere, which is stacked with ornate, stuccoed villas with commanding views of the city. Many were showing worn edges, and others had been beautifully restored in order to house the city's aristocrats. Some, however, had been made into inns and restaurants. Many sat far behind imposing gates as ornate as the houses. The crown atop all this splendor was the magnificent view of Florence as seen from the Piazzale Michelangelo. We had to stop for a photo.

Finally we were on the Chianti Road. The city disappeared behind a southern hill, immediately putting us in the country. Beautiful Palazzi began to dot hilltops, and in the spaces between were farms and vineyards. This was Chianti territory—the region from Florence to Siena, where the wine known to us today as Chianti has been made from the time of the Etruscans.

We stopped at a little restaurant in Spada for some lunch. Anticipating a big dinner at the *fattoria*, we wanted to eat something light. The place seemed to be filled with locals. A huge man, probably in his seventies, issued commands to all the workers from his perch atop a platform overlooking the room. The walls were covered with pictures of him singing or with his arms around what appeared to be celebrities, although we knew none. These photos were of him at a much younger and seemingly happier age. We ordered lightly, and I was able to make out some of his barking commands. He was complaining that we hadn't ordered enough, and the poor waiter encouraged us to order more. The owner made up for our small order by charging us the ever-popular table fee and by serving our four-euro bottle of water with the cap off. The reason for the missing cap was discovered as I watched him pour water from half-used bottles to create a full new bottle for the next victim.

Back on the road, I wanted to stop at Greve, the unofficial capital of Chianti, but our detour in Florence was going to make us late arriving at the *fattoria*. Joyce and I decided we'd rather pass through Greve and make a stop at Villa Vignamaggio, the fourteenth-century villa where Mona Lisa was born in 1479. Its winery has operated for over six hundred years, making some of Chianti's best.

About five kilometers south of Greve, a left turn onto a dirt road took us through a few farms and to the top of a hill, where the pink stucco villa stood amid exquisite gardens that had served as a set for the 1993 production of *Much Ado About Nothing*. The villa is now an inn attached to the winery—part of the thriving agritourism business in Italy. We talked to the proprietor of the winery, who told us an hour-long tour would begin in half an hour and end with a tasting. There wasn't enough time. Only a few days into our trip, we were already experiencing the usual frustration with trying to fit too much in. I guess we hadn't managed to slow down after all. Would we ever? We bought a bottle of their wine, which I knew was excellent from having had it in the United States. Walking back to the car, I took a few photos of our postcard-perfect view of the commanding estate. It seemed to embody the essence of photos always seen of the Tuscan countryside: neat rows of cypress trees leading to stone cottages with tiled roofs resting majestically on the brows of gently rounded hills. One could sit and drink in this view for hours, but we pushed on, ever mindful of that self-imposed timeline.

After laboriously piecing together the maps I had purchased with the directions sent to us, we eventually arrived at the Valdarno exit of the Autostrada. Now I was back on course and could follow the directions, which took us via Route SS69 through an extremely unattractive modern town named Montevarchi. I was amazed that the same society that brought us the Renaissance and the beauty of art, music, and culture could also devise such awful eyesores as these modern towns, which seemed to consist entirely of concrete and metal apartment buildings. This town even had a mall that resembled an abandoned factory; it housed the European version of a combined clothing, jewelry, food, and appliance store, cleverly called COOP. Traffic was horrendous as we inched through this drab, concrete monolith and back out again into open country.

After turning off the main road, we drove through the charming little village of Pergine Valdarno, where we began to see signs for the Fattoria Montelucci. The signs snaked us through the village and onto a dirt road that climbed up a steep hill, making switchback turns as it first passed a few farmhouses, then just wild woodland and sky. As we crested the hill, the *fattoria* came into view below us, a cluster of stone buildings riding a low ridge with views on either side. Off to the distance on our left, we could see hints of the Autostrada miles away and far below, as though we were riding in a plane. To our right were fields of olive trees and grapevines, more hills, and the tiny specks of two distant villages.

Tuscany, the Cooking School, and Unwinding

At 5:00 PM, we rolled onto the gravel parking lot of a long, two-story stone build-ing flanked by stables, a separate main lobby, and a restaurant. A massive, double-arched doorway opened into a large room with stone walls, a wooden floor, and a beamed ceiling far above. To the right, a polished and ornately carved wooden bar ran the length of the room. To the left were loosely arranged tables, a couch, a few lounging chairs, and a table covered with newspapers, books, and bro-chures. The far wall was lined with shelves of wine bottles. In the middle of the wall, a grand open archway led to a set of stairs and down into the restaurant. It was warm and welcoming.

A young, attractive woman smiled and greeted us. A couple that appeared to be around our age sat at a nearby table, the man talking on his cell phone. From their mannerisms, I could tell there was a problem. My intuition told me they were registered for our cooking class, but discretion kept me from making an introduction. Later, we met Bruce and Rachel; they were our cooking partners, and we learned of their problem.

We followed our hostess to our room—outside, behind the building, and down a set of stone stairs notched into the hillside to another low, stone building. Recessed into the thick stone wall were four small, wooden doors, with a tiny window next to each door. At one time, this building had housed stables; now it housed our room. The room was small and dark and smelled of disinfectant. Black bugs scurried across the floor as we entered. The lone window gave the only light.

Trying to remain upbeat as we looked at each other in horror, Joyce com-mented, "This is a charming little room." Visions of those little bugs crawling over us as we tried to fall asleep were disturbing, and it would be impossible to live with that odor for a week.

I politely asked, "Is there another room available—maybe one a little larger, with more windows? And ... there are bugs in here."

She smiled and said with equal politeness, "Certainly. Let us go back and see if anything else is available."

Back at the now-empty bar, our hostess found us another room. It would be in a different building, a little farther from the restaurant. Would we mind the walk? Of course not; we were there for a cooking and walking class! We followed her to the other building to have a look. Back outside, it was obvious the adjoin-ing building had been the main house when this was a farm. It was large, stately, and stuccoed—typical of the Tuscan palazzi we had seen from the road.

"What about a room in this building?" I asked.

"Oh, these are all occupied, except for a few suites that are very expensive. But I'm certain you'll like the room I will show you." We passed a welcoming swimming pool with a drop-dead gorgeous view of the hills beyond. It was a warm day, and three or four people were enjoying the pool.

About fifty yards beyond the pool, I spotted another stone building that probably housed the workers at one time. It was a large stone building, though not as grand as the main house. It was loaded with charm—heavy stone tiered three levels down the sloping grounds, red barrel-tiled roof, several stone chimneys, massive double wooden doors, and wood-framed windows opened to the country air.

We entered a large sitting room with a tiled, beamed ceiling and stucco fireplace. The furniture was of heavy antique class, but comfortable and welcoming. Our room had the same ceiling, and its stone floor was covered by attractive rugs and accessories. A shuttered double window opened to a view of artichoke fields, and beyond, a line of bygone pig or chicken huts. This was much better; we would take it. She left us to unpack and prepare for our welcome dinner.

The walk back to the restaurant was along a stone path lined with cypress trees and an occasional iron lamppost. The evening air was warm, with a soft breeze. As Joyce and I strolled hand in hand to the restaurant, I could feel the tension and need for speed dropping from my shoulders. When we entered the building, we saw some couples at the tables having wine. The hostess greeted us like old friends, asked if we were happy with our room, and led us to our table, where our cooking partners already were seated.

This room had once housed the olive press, and it oozed character. That wonderful stone was everywhere—on the walls, floors, beamed ceiling, and on the massive pillars throughout the room. The middle of the room featured the huge grinding wheel of the press. Ten-foot-tall arched windows along the back wall showered the room with daylight and the magnificent view. Now that evening had fallen, the candlelit room glowed, punctuated by tiny lights glistening in the distance.

Joining Bruce and Rachel at a lovely window-side table, we launched the preliminary get-acquainted conversation and discovered that only the four of us had registered for the class. We were welcomed with an envelope of our itineraries and news that we could choose anything on the dinner menu. Bruce and Rachel were from California, but Bruce had attended a Pittsburgh university, so we had a common bond. We talked of Pittsburgh and California and our impressions of our first day at Montelucci.

Joyce and I discovered that our new friends also disapproved of their room. This was the problem they were dealing with when we first saw them in the lobby. Being first, they had fought that particular battle before we arrived, and had considered leaving. They were told the company that ran the cooking program contracted with the *fattoria* for the cheapest rooms. Bruce had phoned the company, which initially refused to upgrade his room. Calculating the regular room rates for the *fattoria*, Bruce claimed we could be upgraded from standard to deluxe, plus eat anything on the menu, and the company would still make a huge profit. The company agreed, and the *fattoria* management complied. This was being resolved as we registered, so our request for an upgrade was handled easily.

Since Rachel was having physical problems, including difficulty walking, the couple wanted a room near the restaurant. They decided to spend the first two nights in the original room until they could be moved to a nice room in the main house.

The meal was delightful: three hours of decadent gorging on wine and food. We had a bottle of Chianti, a bottle of water, and an antipasto of assorted Sienese cheeses with jam and honey. For the *primo piatto*, Joyce had gnocchetti gratin with pecorino cheese and saffron; I had tortelli of potatoes with truffles. We both chose mixed grilled meats with country fresh salad as our *secondo piatto*. I could barely eat this mouthwatering cuisine without slobbering all over my plate. *Dolce* was a peach tart washed down with an after-dinner wine. By eleven o'clock, we were hoisting ourselves out of our chairs, thankful for the long walk back to the room.

Exhausted and full, we lumbered into our room, threw open the window, and slept as though dead, the cool September breeze waving over our contented bodies. At 4:30 AM, the rooster began to crow outside our window. I got up, closed the window and shutters, and promptly fell back to sleep until eight.

For breakfast, it was back to the restaurant for croissants, breads, meats and cheeses, yogurt, juices, and wonderful cappuccino. We were greeted by the kind, dimpled smile and dark olive eyes of Vera, the motherly breakfast hostess/cappuccino maker who also would be the chef's aide in our cooking classes. As I reached for a croissant, my elbow hit the decanter of orange juice, which fell and shattered on the stone floor. As I picked up the shards of glass, Vera sauntered over and, gently waving me off, started cleaning up the mess. I was embarrassed, and in my best attempt at the language, repeated several times, "*Mi di spiace*" (I'm sorry).

Vera touched my arm and with the gentlest smile said, "*Non problema, tranquilla, tranquilla.*" Vera didn't speak a word of English, but she enjoyed my rough attempts at Italian and, after this bit of bonding, talked directly to me as though I could understand every word. I must admit, we did communicate well … or at least we thought we did.

After breakfast, Joyce and I started on our first hike. It was to be a seven-kilometer walk to the eleventh-century walled-hill town of Civitella, where we would lunch in a trattoria before hiking back. Because of Rachel's problem, she and Bruce would drive to meet us at the trattoria.

The September morning was crystal clear and warm enough for shorts and sandals. Following our packet directions, Joyce and I took a meandering dirt road along a ridge that offered a view of the Tuscan countryside for miles. The silence was so peaceful. I thought, *I could live here.* I felt so at home passing through fallow fields; I could imagine moving into one of the abandoned farmhouses and staying awhile among the grape vines, olive trees, and patches of wild roses sporting huge rose hips. On the entire walk, only two cars passed us. At one point, we came upon a shrine—a little stone alcove big enough for us to stand in, with a tiny altar warded by a Virgin Mary statue and appointed with a votive candle and fresh flowers. Joyce added field flowers to the vase. Farther along, a scrawny black kitten joined us for a mile of our walk.

Rounding a bend, I spotted the walled village of Civitella in the distance, clinging to a hillside with its jagged cap of *castello* tower ruins. It was lovelier than a fantasy Disney village. I took photos and stood admiring its beauty.

The road stretched on, winding through olive orchards and past two stately homes that sat behind gates outfitted with security lights and speaker systems. Wealthy dwellers of Florence or Siena had discovered the charm of this countryside and were buying these modest farms to build trophy-mansion retreats. I hoped these developments would not ruin the natural beauty, although the heavy hand of the newly affluent often did.

As the dirt road twisted along the ridge, Civitella came in and out of view, each time growing closer. At last, there it was, looming large and inviting, on the hill opposite us. We only had to walk down the hill and up the other side, then up the steep stone steps leading through the entry. Once inside, we found ourselves in a deserted, tiny square, with the magnificent valley view behind us and buildings surrounding us: a beauty parlor, a café with a few outside tables, and an alimentary (tiny grocery or general store).

It was quiet, like a ghost town, although well kept and pleasant. Great care had been taken of the polished wooden doors of these little stone homes all stacked on each other. With no space for gardens, owners had planted climbing flowering plants that totally encompassed their doorways. Everything was in full bloom. At an intersection of two narrow lanes, a grotto had been carved into the stone wall of a building to house a statue of Mary.

We continued up several stepped alleyways to the top of the village, which opened into a larger square. To our right was a steepled church, in the middle was a large well, and to our left was the castello, its grounds now a park sprinkled with modern sculpture. Running between the two structures and along the back of the square was an arcaded street. Walking up this street, we came upon an open door surrounded by posters. A sign over the door read *La Storia*. We stopped to look and discovered this was Civitella's little museum. There was not a soul in sight.

Inside were photos and cases of objects, each carefully labeled in Italian and English. Intrigued, we wandered through this little room, reading about the horror this peaceful-looking village had experienced during World War II.

On June 29, 1944, Herbert Goring and his Nazi troops marched into the village. Along the way, two German soldiers had been shot and killed. Goring ordered every man eighteen years of age and older to be brought into the square in front of the church. He announced that ten Italian men would be shot for every German killed, and the women and children must stay to watch. He began by ordering men to be shot in the head five at a time. In his enthusiasm, he killed all 161 men before ceasing the orders. Then the guards were sent into houses to kill any women and children who had not come out to witness this horror. After performing this grisly task, the troops set the town on fire and left.

British troops headed by Captain Morgan later entered the village and nursed many of the wounded back to health, buried the dead, and helped clean up the devastation.

We walked out into the sunlight and to the church, which was flanked by plaques bearing the names of all who had died in this tragedy, as well as the names of the British soldiers who helped them. Standing in the brilliant daylight, looking over this lovely village adorned with flowers and works of art, I pondered how mankind could commit such atrocities. These people were so kind and pleasant. How could they have recovered? Our papers are full of stories of bitterness and vengeful acts that are far less traumatic. I thought about the petty issues that distressed me from day to day. How meaningless they seemed.

Sobered by this experience, we walked to the Antico Borgo and met Bruce and Rachel. This little restaurant had also once housed an olive press. Stone floors and walls, a beamed ceiling, and remnants of the old press made this small room cool and refreshing. The floors above housed an inn, with the top level opening onto the main square. There were no other people in the place. A nice woman greeted us and seated us at a "reserved" table backed by a ledge in the wall loaded with wine bottles. We were served a delectable meal of gnudi (a type of gnocchi made from ricotta cheese and spinach) topped with pecorino, cream, and pears; then pennette with bell peppers and pancetta; followed by duck breast and salt cod on Swiss chard. For *dolce*, we had cantuccini, which are Tuscan biscotti dipped in an exquisite dessert wine called Vin Santo. The meal was a pure delight.

On the walk back, our friend the kitten rejoined us, along with a brother and sister. They followed us all the way back to the *fattoria*. After that huge meal, the walk seemed all uphill.

As we were hot and dusty and tired from our eleven-mile hike, the pool looked inviting. Joyce sat at one of the chaises; I dove in and thought I heard someone scream. It was me. The water was spring fed—and ice-cold. Once my heart resumed beating, the water felt refreshing. The setting sun cast brilliant shafts of rose and pink across an autumn sky. Long shadows formed over the hills and valley below. We were in heaven, looking down on some of the most beautiful countryside in the world.

After that glorious sunset, it was back to the room to shower and dress for dinner. Yes, it was already time for another huge meal. Why was no one overweight with all this eating? Was it because of the walking? For our sake, I hoped that was the case.

The meal started with salade di Medici, which was a tantalizing mélange of greens, pine nuts, white grapes, and chunks of pecorino and apple. The dressing was a mix of olive oil, balsamic vinegar, and honey, resulting in a wonderful treat. We skipped the *primo* and went straight to the *secondo*. Tonight, we would dine on what Tuscany is famous for: grilled beefsteak. The chef carried a butcher knife and huge chunk of steak to the table on a wooden cutting board. After we each chose the size of piece we preferred, the chef cut it at the table for our approval before taking it to be grilled. The chef who performed this drama would be our teacher at the morning cooking class.

This chef, Alessandro Bettini, was the handsome embodiment of the Italian stereotype. He could be no more than thirty years old, and he sported a diamond stud in his nose and an earring in one ear. His face was framed by tight, curly black hair and a tiny, squared goatee. He wore a crisp white double-breasted jacket with black-and-white paisley collar and cuffs to match his slacks and black apron. His perky swagger and endearing smile could charm the toughest customer. Alessandro chose three wines and had them served with his compliments to accompany our meal. The melt-in-your-mouth succulent steaks were adorned with the most delicious roasted potatoes I'd ever tasted. The whole experience was orgasmic. We waddled to our room at eleven o'clock for a sound sleep in total silence and solitude.

The next morning, Vera cheerfully greeted us with wonderful hot cappuccinos. After breakfast, she ushered us into the kitchen, where Allesandro, today clad in white attire and a large work handkerchief over his hair, was busy preparing for our lesson.

The kitchen was bright and operating-room clean. The long, narrow room had tile floors and white tile walls. Ample industrial lighting illuminated stainless steel gas stoves with massive ventilation hoods and wall ovens running the length of the room. Down the center was a long, stainless steel–topped worktable, where we took our stations and Alessandro did his preparations. At one end of the room was a window with a great view of the Tuscan countryside. At the other end was a door leading to the vegetable and herb garden, where Alessandro clipped fresh ingredients for each dish.

We were given white aprons and notepaper. Today's lesson was on fresh pasta, duck sauce, and apple cake. Always smiling, Alessandro went to extra lengths to make sure we were getting what we wanted in instruction. He carefully weighed each ingredient to give accurate recipes. However, all measurements were in grams and would have to be converted when we got home. Alessandro did all the work. We took notes, asked questions, and performed minor chores, such as stirring the pot on the stove and chopping vegetables. Bruce videotaped the entire session. Time flew in the laid-back atmosphere.

Vera cleaned utensils as Alessandro finished with them, and she made dough for the pasta. The two of them worked well in concert, with Alessandro skillfully switching between Italian with Vera and English with us. He patiently answered all of our questions, some of which were terribly irrelevant. He also gave us a little history of the place. We knew Montelucci was still a working farm. He told us there were two thousand olive trees on the property, yielding one thousand liters of olive oil per year.

At the end of the lesson, Vera served garlic cloves marinated in olive oil, vinegar, and rosemary; olives; bread; and spumanti. She and Alessandro joined us in a toast; we took photos, and she led us to our seats in the restaurant while Alessandro finished cooking the meal we had started. Vera served it with more wine, and that was our lunch.

The afternoon schedule featured a drive to Montalcino for a tour and tasting at the Barbi winery—home of the coveted Brunello di Montalcino, purported to be the finest wine in all of Italy. Vera had told me to stop at two villages on the way. One was famous for its pecorino cheese and the other for truffle oil. In the

United States, you almost need to take out a mortgage to buy truffle oil, but it was really cheap in Italy, so Joyce wanted to load up.

Unfortunately, we got lost and never found either village. (It certainly couldn't have been the result of any miscommunication between Vera and me.) But we didn't get to Montalcino until nearly four o'clock, and our tour of the winery was scheduled for five, so that didn't leave much time to see the village. This was unfortunate, because Montalcino is a charming thirteenth-century, walled hill town.

We parked the car and walked a few streets, managing to find our way to the castello at the top of the town. Castellos are fortified castles that were usually built at the strategic tops of these Italian hill towns by the warring ruling families. The streets of Montalcino were about as wide as alleys and were lined with wine shops and small clothing and gift stores. The *castello* was intact and now housed an *enoteca*, or wine bar. It would be a great place to sit, enjoy the 360-degree view, and sip some of the delicious, very expensive Brunello. Instead, we ran into a COOP and bought bottled water.

I must comment on the honesty of these people. Parking was at a premium, so each of the few free parking spaces in town carried a strict time limit. Prominent signs warned the driver of a ticket if the limit were exceeded. How did they track the time a car was parked? The driver was instructed to write the time of arrival on a piece of paper and leave it on the dashboard. Could you see that working in the United States? Perhaps it didn't work here either, but no one seemed to care.

Sadly, we soon had to leave Montalcino and drive to the Castello di Barbi. It was an enchanting place. Obviously, the vintner families have made some money through the years. Unlike in the American culture, generation after generation live in the family house, each one adding a wing or additional floors and placing pieces of sculpture throughout the yard. If this tradition lasted long enough, the family home became quite impressive, loaded with history and charm. This was the case at Castello di Barbi. Various wings or buildings each revealed evidence of a different era and bits of family history.

Rachel and Bruce had not arrived by the designated tour time. We participated in the tour and tasting without knowing what had happened to them. The Brunello di Montalcino lived up to everything I had learned about it. What a glorious wine! Even with the dollar taking a beating from the euro, we bought a few bottles for less than they cost in the United States. Walking out of the tasting room, we encountered Rachel and Bruce. They were very upset. The directions in our packet were not good; they also had gotten lost and had been driving around the Tuscan countryside the whole time, not enjoying it at all. They were hot and tired, and the place was closing.

True to what we had learned about Italian hospitality so far on this trip, the people at the winery were sympathetic of their story and graciously took them on a tour of their own, followed by a tasting, even though it was after closing time. Joyce and I told them to enjoy their tour and left in pursuit of the truffle oil. This time, we found Castiglione d'Orta, the village Vera had recommended. It was a tiny, medieval hilltop village. (I was fast coming to understand that in Italy, every town is a tiny, medieval hill town.) We had to take a steep and narrow winding road to get there. It was getting dark, and this little detour was taking us further from the *fattoria*. I was tired. All this for some oil I might not be able to fit into my suitcase or legally take into the country.

By the time we reached the center of town, night had fallen, and everything was closed or closing. Joyce spied a tiny alimentary still open. We ran in and found two bottles of the stuff for 3.50 euros—a bargain, and certainly worth the trip in Joyce's eyes.

Now we had to find our way home. It had taken more than two and a half hours to get to Montalcino, even though the directions said it would be a half hour. We were now even farther away and had no idea how we had gotten there. Searching the map, Joyce discovered we could go a little farther east and get on the Autostrada. That would cut considerable time off the trip. Why hadn't they just told us to do this? The Autostrada took us north of the *fattoria*. We got off at Valdarno and had to backtrack. After a two-hour drive, we arrived at the *fattoria* at nine thirty, ran into the restaurant, and had our dinner. We ate light and then strolled the grounds, immersed in the romance of a star-filled September sky accented with the shimmering lights of a distant village.

In the morning, we awoke refreshed and walked to the restaurant, ready for our next cooking lesson. Greeted by the ever-cheerful Vera and smiling Alessandro, we were asked if we would like to make anything in particular. Joyce and Rachel both said they would like to know how to make gnudi, the ricotta and spinach gnocchi eaten at Civitella. He agreed and changed the menu right there. We would start by making a chicken liver pâté, then gnudi (this time served with pecorino cheese and truffle oil), followed by crème di ceci (chickpea soup) garnished with squid-ink noodles. The class was great. Allesandro couldn't have been more helpful and accommodating. Because of his limited English, he took extra care to make certain we understood him.

He explained that *gnudi* meant "nude." Gnudi was actually similar to the stuffing of ravioli, but without the "clothes"—the pasta covering. First, he drained the liquid of ricotta made from sheep's milk and spooned it into a bowl. Then he added grated Parmesan cheese, finely chopped spinach, and three egg yolks. To lightly coat the mixture, he grated a little nutmeg, along with salt, pepper, and a handful of flour. He put the mixture into a pastry bag, then squeezed and cut the dough into nuggets the size of a thumb tip. The nuggets were dropped into a pot of boiling water for a few minutes, then scooped out and put into ice water to stop the cooking. He spooned the cooled gnudi into individual ceramic bowls; sprinkled them with Parmesan cheese, a little fresh ground pepper, and truffle oil; and popped them in the oven for five minutes. They were a true gourmet treat.

For the end-of-lesson celebration, Vera prepared three types of bruschetti: one type with bacon, another with olive oil and garlic, and the other with olives and rosemary. Alessandro opened a bottle of prosecco, a wonderful sparkling wine from the Veneto region of northern Italy. We toasted a great class, took photos, and exchanged promises to return. Next, we headed for the restaurant to eat the fruits of our labor.

In the afternoon, we drove to the village of Radda, one of three centers that form the first designated Chianti wine region. We needed to buy a travel-sized clothing iron, which we had forgotten, and an alarm clock to replace our broken one. So we stopped at the COOP in Montevarchi. The place was hideous—American fast food, discount shopping, and supermarket all rolled into one huge post-World War II industrial building, the height of ugliness. After leaving the beauty and serenity of our country haven, it was like being shot back to a Super Wal-Mart—one of my most disturbing nightmares. We got in and out as quickly as possible.

The drive to Radda was beautiful; the road wound over hills and through valleys dotted with farms and stone houses. Radda came into view from a distance, cascading over a hill. We were becoming blasé to these storybook villages; they were all beginning to look alike. Yet my heart still raced upon seeing each one. Radda, an eleventh-century fortified town, had a charming park dominated by a fountain—a tribute to some hero we didn't know. There were the usual narrow stone streets, with some tunneling under others, and the occasional grotto to Mary. Scaffolding on many of the buildings suggested a great deal of reconstruction. We must have been suffering from charming-village overload, for we spent little time here. Instead, we headed out of town for Castello d'Albola, one of the quintessential Chianti Classico wineries.

The Chianti region covers about sixty-five square miles between Florence and Siena and was the first officially designated wine-producing area in the world.

Many other wines are labeled as Chianti, but only the government-approved wineries in this region may use the coveted "Chianti Classico" name. After touring the town on our own, we were to go to one of the premier wineries of Chianti Classico for a tour and tasting.

The *castello* sat at the top of a steep hill covered with grapevines; at the top was a panoramic view of Chianti country. The winery itself, was comprised of a cluster of fourteenth-century buildings. Also on the property was an eleventh-century castle—the original family home.

We toured the winery and cellars and learned that the facility was one of the largest in Italy, exporting 80 percent of their wine. They also made olive oil. After the tour, we had a tasting of both. Olive-oil tasting is interesting. It is done in the same manner as wine in that the taster slowly sniffs it, then takes a mouthful and swishes it around in the mouth before swallowing. It really burned going down my throat and didn't taste very good. Our guide explained that Tuscan olive oil is peppery and strong compared to others. This was said with great pride. However, we decided to stick to wine tasting and save the olive oil for our salads. Since Castello d'Albola wine is readily available at home and is not impressive, we did not buy any. We would purchase only good wines we could not get at home.

Walking from the courtyard to the parking area, I noticed an ominous black wall of clouds forming. I took a quick photo, and then we jumped into the car and headed back to the *fattoria*. The storm broke in all its fury, which slowed our progress. Joyce complained of pain—the beginning of a bladder infection. We had no medicine for it and had more than three weeks left. What should we do?

When we reached Pergin Valdarno, I stopped at a pharmacy. The pharmacist did not speak English, so I tried to explain our situation in my fractured Italian. He apparently understood and told us she needed amoxicillin. As I explained we had no prescription, he pulled a box out of a drawer and indicated the price—four euros. Shocked, I paid him, and we left. Afterward, I thought we should have bought a case. We could have made a fortune in the States—right before going to jail.

Back at the *fattoria*, we freshened up and headed for dinner. The weather had changed. The wind was whipping rain in our faces, and the temperature had dropped. Sweaters and an umbrella could not keep out the chill. Once inside the cozy warmth of the restaurant, we enjoyed another wonderful meal and more wine. As we were leaving, Alessandro and the manager of the *fattoria* spent time talking with us, and the manager let Joyce e-mail the kids on her computer. The entire staff was so friendly and cheerful. This was truly a warm and welcoming place.

I spent the rest of the night trying to figure out how to use our new, futuristic, "one button for all settings" alarm clock, following the Italian directions.

On Saturday morning—our last full day at Montelucci—Vera told us about nearby Monte San Salvino, with its wonderful ceramics. Joyce wanted to buy some Italian ceramics, and Vera assured us this was the place. Even though this was to be our second hiking day, we decided to drive. The change in the weather meant the air would be uncomfortably cold, and the winding dirt road out of the *fattoria* would be a sea of mud. Besides, the directions were confusing, and we did not want to be wandering about lost on foot.

We reached Monte San Salvino easily and found the shop Vera had recommended, Giotto. The showroom out front displayed exquisite pieces by the Giotto family. I never even thought to ask if they were related to the famous painter, but their work was the most beautiful I'd seen. Unfortunately, it was also very expensive. The people were gracious and patient. They explained patterns, answered our questions, and even took us back into the workshop where they made all their pieces, pointing out work done by the uncle or the brother or one or another family member.

After we narrowed our choices to two pieces, they calculated the shipping, which would have been more than 100 euros. Each piece was nearly 500 euros (in the current exchange rate, more than $600) without shipping. At those prices, the original Giotto must have made them. They suggested we could save on shipping by carrying our acquisition home. I could envision my arrival in the United States with these beautiful works of art in a million pieces. I told them we were just starting out and would stop by on our way home. They were so gracious that we felt guilty for taking their time, but we fully intended to return.

From San Salvino, we took a short drive to the village of Pieve a Presciano for a private tour and tasting paired with various foods at the Fattoria di Presciano. We arrived an hour early, but could not find the *fattoria*. This was a small village and, after circling it three times, we went into a tiny alimentary to ask directions. No one spoke English, but once again, they made a great effort trying to give us directions. The kind lady kept saying "*sempre adestra*"—always right. So it was back into the car, turning right at every intersection, and there it was. We had been driving past it, because there was no sign.

This was another of the many hidden jewels of this trip: a huge, L-shaped, two-story building built in the fourteenth century as a farm. The first floor was of stone, the second of brick. It featured massive arched wooden doors, walls covered with climbing vines, and an entrance courtyard enclosed by a stone wall and graced with massive iron gates. Across a small dirt lane, grape fields alternated with cypress trees and pines.

A small group of people were finishing a tour and browsing the wine shelves. One couple heard us speak English and introduced themselves. Originally from Arizona, they were retired and lived in Sun City, near Phoenix. Their daughter, an artist living in Tuscany, owned a shop in Cortona, and they were on their way to visit her. We had a delightful conversation, and they gave us their card and invited us to contact them if we ever found ourselves in Phoenix.

The group left, and we met the owner, a young man named Pasquale Cometti. He was originally from the region of Veneto and, in 1991, had gone to Florence to study wine making. After deciding to stay in Tuscany, he and his wife bought this place in 1999. At the time, the property was in total ruin and had to be completely rebuilt. They now had seventy-four acres of grapes and made 900,000 bottles a year of five different wines, grappa, and Vin Santo. Pasquale had won awards and was most proud of them. He asked if we would like to start the tour.

Once again, Rachel and Bruce were not there. It was late, and our designated time with him was from noon to three, when the *fattoria* closed for the lunch period. We decided to tour without our friends. Pasquale personally took us through the cellars and bottling area. He spoke limited English, but gave a most informative tour. By the time we returned to the store, his wife had set a beautiful table of meats, cheeses, breads, olives, and delicious flat bread topped with tomatoes, oregano, and olive oil.

As we were about to begin the tasting, Rachel and Bruce arrived, agitated. They had gotten lost and had just found the place. They were angry at the company for giving such poor directions, angry at this owner for not having a sign, and just plain angry in general. They planned to do battle with the American company that had put our cooking and walking class together, and were going to ask for a refund upon returning home. Joyce and I really felt badly for them and agreed certain aspects were poorly done. We had signed up because it was open-ended and allowed for more freedom than other options. And it was less expensive. That said, there was evidence of poor planning and a lack of attention to detail, and I would send them a critical evaluation once back home.

We got past all that and into enjoying the sumptuous feast Mrs. Cometti had prepared. Before starting the food, Pasquale poured a spumante as an aperitif. Then he poured four different reds, from the youngest to the oldest, each to be drank with one of the delicious foods. He explained and gave evaluations of each wine, suggesting foods for each. This wonderful tasting ended with Vin Santo, a special dessert wine the Tuscans serve with biscotti. They dip the biscotti into the wine with great joy. We bought two of his reds and a bottle of Vin Santo, thanked him and his lovely wife for a more-than-memorable experience, and started back to Montelucci.

Once at the *fattoria*, we walked through the stables and around the grounds. Eventually, we headed back to our room to pack, feeling a little sad. This was our last night here. This friendly little retreat was cocooned in a peaceful, safe feeling. It had come to feel like home. At the end of our evening meal, Alessandro came out of the kitchen and gave the four of us a glass of liquor made by monks from a friary in the mountains near Arezzo. He said it was for special occasions and toasted us. We thanked him for the great lessons and invited him to visit us in the States. Everyone shook hands, and he promised to take us up on our offer in two years. Planning to get on the road early in the morning, we said our good-byes to Alessandro, Bruce, and Rachel.

After waking up with the rooster and packing the car, we had an early breakfast. Vera was especially attentive. We thanked her for being a most gracious hostess. She kissed Joyce and me on each cheek, hugged us tightly, and wished us well. This would be an experience I would never forget. It felt as though we were leaving family to go out on our own. Climbing into the car, we waved good-bye, feeling a little sad about leaving this tranquil paradise of friendly people. We were off to Cortona.

Falling in Love with Venice; Finding Saint Anthony

We were told Cortona had an antique fair the last Sunday of every month, and after reading *Under the Tuscan Sun* and seeing the movie, we wanted to make a stop, even though it would take us out of our way. We were en route to Venice, but thought, "It's a small country; it won't hurt to make this little detour." However, in order to see Cortona, we would have to scrap our visit to Arezzo.

The ride to Cortona was a feast for the eyes. Every hill had a village perched upon its brow, and yet each was different and held out an invitation to visit and explore. Of course, there was not enough time. Our next trip here would definitely be devoted entirely to staying in the country and exploring villages not on the typical tour company list.

Cortona is one of the oldest towns in Italy and was one of the twelve cities of the Etruscan League. Clinging to its own hill, it offered dramatic views out over a wide, fertile valley and Lake Trasimeno in the distance. After climbing a very steep winding road with no guardrails, we arrived at a small piazza dominated by that commanding view. Cars had to be parked on the street outside the town walls, where tickets were purchased for the estimated length of the stay and displayed on the windshield. The streets inside the town walls were no wider than alleyways and were pedestrian only, except for deliveries. All the side streets were merely stone stairs going up from one side or down from the other. People living here had to have a great sense of balance.

The main town square was familiar to us from having seen it in the movie—and, more recently, in an Andréa Rue concert broadcast over PBS. Aside from the thrill of being in this place we had seen so many times, the square was actually fairly uninspiring. Everything was grey stone and stark. It was well preserved from its ancient past, but not visually inspiring. The buildings were plain, and aside from the steps up the front of the municipal building, there was no place to sit. We saw no charming cafés, just many cheap souvenir stores and crowds of tour-bus people. There also was no sign of an antique fair.

Asking around about the fair, all we could glean was that nothing was happening this particular Sunday. On the way up the hill, we had seen the church of Santa Maria Grazzie, which was shown in the movie and photographed often in publications about Cortona. There really wasn't any more to see in Cortona, and since it was Sunday, we drove down to the church for a visit.

The church, like the town, was a beautiful jewel from a distance, but rather stark and disappointing inside. On the door was the mass schedule; one was due to begin. We decided to stay. There must have been ten people in the church. The priest came by and asked if we were there for mass. I answered yes. He told us to follow him.

Joyce asked, "What did he say?"

I said, "I think he asked if we were staying for mass. I said yes, and he said we should follow him."

"Where are we going?"

"I don't know … maybe the mass is in a back room, since there are so few people."

But he walked behind the altar and into the sacristy (the room where priests robe for mass). There were other people in the room who seemed to know each other and appeared to be busy preparing for mass.

"Why did he want us in here?" asked Joyce. "Do you think we're going to have to do something?" I asked one of the men, and he smiled and seemed to say something like, "Don't worry. We'll tell you what to do." Just then, the priest was ready to start the procession. Everyone lined up. The man handed Joyce a key on a velvet pillow—the key to the tabernacle. He handed me a gold dish holding the Host. An altar boy walked over to a large rope hanging from the ceiling in the corner of the room and labored at pulling on it, which brought the large bell in the tower to life with a tinny clanging as we proceeded to the altar, placed the articles on a table, and took our seats. It was a lovely mass with beautiful singing. We were glad to have been a part of it.

After mass, we started our drive to Venice. Cortona was surprisingly close to the Autostrada. We were soon on it and driving at 130 kilometers per hour for Venice. I love driving the Autostrada. It is possible to make great time, because everyone follows a certain etiquette. Slower cars stay in the right lane. They only use the left lane to pass, then quickly move back into the right lane. No one passes on the right, and no one hogs the left lane. If someone is in the left lane, an approaching car will dip its lights; the slower car moves right, and the fast one zooms by without ever having to touch the brake. This is my kind of driving! And the police are not hovering at every underpass, waiting to pounce on any car going a few miles over the speed limit. To illustrate this point, I saw the greatest sign on the Autostrada while traveling on a six-lane stretch. The speed limit was 90 km, and right next to the speed sign was another that read "Left lane for 120 km or greater."

I had to stop for gas and realized for the first time that the car had a diesel engine. Diesel fuel was 1.4 euros per liter—nearly seven dollars a gallon. The rest stops on the Autostrada are wonderful. They have fairly nice restaurants and fast food—except that their fast food is good food. Not even the cheapest order includes fried burgers, french fries, or stale coffee. These stops employ cooks to prepare gnocchi and other pastas; a large selection of sandwiches made of prosciutto or hot *paninis*; olives; salads; and wine in drink dispensers similar to the American soda fountain, which is actually a great concept. They also sell gifts and groceries, and they feature huge, very clean restrooms. These restrooms have a resident attendant keeping them clean, and there is a strategically placed basket for donations which are expected, not suggested. Italian rest stops are actually enjoyable. So while we were stopped for gas, we got some prosciutto sandwiches and stretched our legs a little, then got back on the road, ready to make some time.

The ride took us through a mosaic of scenery. First we saw the low, gentler hills of Tuscany, crowned with hill towns or castellos; approaching Florence, the hills became a little steeper, with fine villas replacing the old ruins of castellos. Through the broad river valley of Florence, heavy traffic and industrialization dominated. No sooner had the valley started than we were out of it, journeying into a much steeper and more dramatic climb into the mountains of Emilia Romano. What a marvel these Italian engineers were! The road would swing dramatically out over steep gorges and then back in and through tunnel after tunnel, winding and going up and down, in and out; I couldn't take it all in. Eventually, we dropped out of the mountains into a broad, fertile valley plane. Farmers rode on tractors, working the soil; squat, square stone farmhouses, very different in style from those we had seen in Tuscany, sat alone in the middle of fields. Large stretches of water surrounded by elevated grass walkways abounded outside of Bologna. These were rice fields; we were in risotto country. In the distance, the Dolomites rose majestically into the sky and through the clouds. Our son Paul's in laws had come from that region and spoke of its beauty, but no words could have prepared us for its magnificence upon first sight.

I had made reservations from home for a bed and breakfast in Venice. In our e-mail correspondence, the owner told me to park in Mestra and take the train into Venice. Parking at the Pizzale Roma in Venice was twenty euros a day, compared to five a day at the Garage Mondial in Mestra plus one more euro for a ten-minute train ride. Four hours after leaving Cortona, we pulled into the garage in Mestra, parked, grabbed our luggage, and walked across the street to the train station. There I bought two train tickets and a phone card. I called the bed and breakfast, as instructed in our e-mail, and told them we were at Mestra and would be there within the hour.

Mestra was an ugly, industrial town, and the train ride was through heavy industry and shipyards, then across the very long causeway out to the train station at Venice. The Venice station was big, dirty, and noisy. There were hundreds of tourists everywhere: sitting on the floor, waiting in horrendous lines, and hurriedly walking in all directions. We wove our way through this chaos and out into sunlight and the glorious Grand Canal.

We had been to Venice before, but that first sight of the Grand Canal never ceases to excite. The imitations at Disney and Las Vegas can do wonders, but they can never come close to the drama of the real thing. Like the train station, the canal was filled with a sort of controlled chaos, but in a magnificent setting. It seemed unreal, as though we were on a Hollywood movie set—three-dimensional, yet unreal nonetheless. These proud buildings, a mixture of Eastern, Baroque, and Moorish, came alive before us like strokes of the master painters' brushes. Bridges arched over the canal; boats of all sizes, shapes, and colors moved in every direction without accidents, stopped at little awninged stations similar to bus kiosks, or glided in and out of side canals. Hundreds of people walked over the bridges, jumping on and off boats. These boats barely stopped before switching direction, engines churning up water as they glided back away from the docks they had just approached.

We bought two tickets and got in line for the next *vapparetto*, the Venetian equivalent of a bus on water: a large, barge like flat-bottomed boat with a flat roof and outside deck. Our *vapparetto* glided into the stop, loaded to sinking with people. As some jumped off, we stepped on, squeezing into a space along the guardrail, luggage clutched in our hands. Quickly, the boat pulled away, and we were gliding down the Grand Canal, past magnificent old palazzi. These areas featured glorious architecture, and remained romantically beautiful despite peeling stucco, fading, and sinking. They revealed a glorious past filled with mystery and intrigue.

I have talked with people who told me they didn't like Venice; it smelled, and the buildings were crumbling and sinking into the water. Why didn't they see what I saw, smell what I smelled? Yes, it was old and crumbling, but that was what gave it an air of mystery and a charm that was magnetic. Yes, it smelled, but the smell was of water and fish and centuries of activity, of vendors shouting out their wares for sale, of people on the move. Yes, it was sinking, but the waters engulfing it had brought and sent merchants and seafarers through years of exploration and adventure. Now, as I looked out over the water, thousands of little diamonds were being bounced by the sun over the surface. Tourists glided by in gondolas; workers passed in barges. I sensed mystery, excitement, and an oddly pleasant cacophony that made the heart race. Why hadn't they seen this, felt this?

Our *vapparetto* let us off at station San Stae in the Santa Croce section of the city, where we walked down a *calle*, or narrow lane, then over a little bridge and alongside a narrow canal. Finally, we turned into an even tighter calle that was just shoulder wide, then walked about a block to our address. We were deep in the bowels of everyday Venice. On our previous visit, we had stayed in the heart of the tourist crush and had done all the tourist things: visiting museums, galleries, and churches. But our current area was no tourist attraction. I was thinking this could be a very intimidating place to walk through at night but didn't want to say anything to frighten Joyce.

We encountered a big, heavy wooden door centered with a brass lion's-head knob—and, next to it, three buzzers. I pressed the one marked with our B&B's name, and we were buzzed into a little dark entry with peeling paint on the walls. As we started up the dingy flight of stairs, a light clicked on with the loud echoing clack of an automatic switch, a door above opened, and a petite, impeccably dressed woman with dyed blond hair fashioned into a bouffant poked her head over the railing and instructed us to climb up to her.

As is often the case in Venice, nothing is as it initially appears. One flight up, we entered an elegant, immaculately kept apartment with glasslike, shining terrazzo floors, twelve-foot frescoed ceilings, and handsomely carved and polished wooden doors. We were ushered into a grand salon. At one end was a sitting room with a TV, a fireplace with a menorah on the mantel, and a desk holding a computer. The other end was dominated by an elaborate Venetian crystal chandelier and a mural painted on the wall. This was the dining area, where we would have breakfast. The long table there could comfortably seat eight. A china cupboard held what appeared to be very special pieces: glasses, dishes, and vases, all handsomely painted. Several looked like very expensive Venetian glass.

Our hostess introduced us to a woman who was working at the computer as her daughter, but did not give a name, then took us to our room. Just before a set of glass doors were two doors—one to her bedroom and one to the kitchen. We followed her through the double glass doors and down a hall flanked by three other rooms. This was the entire guest area: four rooms in one end of what had been a grand apartment. She now lived in just one corner while renting out the rest. I wondered what this woman's story was. She never even told us her name, and it was not on any literature or correspondence. This led me to fantasize, as I so often do, about her life.

Perhaps her husband was an entrepreneur or diplomat who had lived larger than life, dying and leaving her in debt, and now she had to rent rooms to keep from losing the place. Or maybe she never married. Perhaps she had been the lover of a wealthy Venetian, bearing his illegitimate child and being forced to live in secrecy in this neighborhood. Perhaps he had died, leaving her penniless, and now she needed the rental income, because she was estranged from her family and had no other income. But then she did tell me she worked outside the home. What was her story? I was certain it had to be interesting; sadly, I was never to find out.

Our room was of modest size, but very well furnished and spotlessly clean. It featured highly polished wooden floors, a Venetian chandelier over the bed; a mural of Raphael's sixteenth-century Sistine Madonna cherubs on the wall behind the bed; and tall, shuttered windows that opened to a view of the shoulder-wide alley below and offered a great view of the inside of the apartment across from us. Our required private bath sported another large window—this one mercifully frosted.

Once we were inside the room, she handed me a piece of paper typed in English titled "Rules of the House," which she proceeded to explain as I read along. This impressive list included instructions on how to enter the building. Specifically, if we were to enter after ten in the evening, we were to ring the buzzer once before entering. We were to be out of our room by a specified time in the morning, so that the maid could clean it without the annoyance of our presence; and each time we departed, we were to leave it in decent condition: clothes hung up, nothing on the floors. There were also instructions on opening and closing the windows and every other consideration an obsessive-compulsive person could want. Why did I feel like a college student visiting my grandmother for the weekend?

After unpacking and freshening up, we went out to explore our neighborhood and other sections of the city. We walked to the Rialto Bridge. The area was teeming with excitement. The canal was very busy; the shop-lined bridge was packed with tourists. Stalls lining the approach to the bridge were spilling over with everything from food and water to clothing and cheap souvenirs. The sides of the Grand Canal around the bridge were lined with restaurants with outdoor seating. One glance at the menus posted at each place confirmed our hostess's recommendation that we instead seek out the much smaller, more charming, and more reasonable places closer to our hotel.

As we walked around the Santa Croce and San Polo neighborhoods, I tried to follow a map and keep a mental note of our path. Venice is a very confusing labyrinth of little alleys that twist and turn and cross over tiny canals and intersect other little alleys. It is quite mysterious and very easy to get lost in. I had often read that part of the charm of Venice was wandering this labyrinth and getting lost, thus finding little jewels that otherwise may not have been experienced. I just hoped one of those jewels wasn't a robbery.

We came upon a small campo flanked by three *osterias*, each with outside seating. This seemed like the area our hostess had recommended. The prices certainly were much more reasonable. Joyce and I chose one of these, taking outside seats and enjoying a great meal with wine and water for twenty-four euros, including cover and tip.

On our way back toward the Rialto after dinner, we noticed people going into the church San Giacomo di Rialto. A sign out front advertised a Vivaldi concert for nineteen euros. We decided to go in and were treated to a rich experience as a string quartet and a soprano performed numbers from Vivaldi, Verdi, and Mozart in the most excellent acoustics surrounded by exquisite statues and works of art. By ten thirty, we were walking back to our room, completely relaxed and consumed by the mysterious beauty of this enchanting city. These dark alleys, although seemingly sinister, were still filled with couples ambling along hand in hand. It was magical.

We rang the bell once and walked up the stairs. The light clacked on, and we were greeted by a whispered hello from our surrogate grandmother, who then turned out the light and retreated back into her room as we quietly slipped past her and into ours. Upon tiptoeing into our room, we noticed that she had gone in while we were out, closed the suitcases we had left open on the floor, and placed them in the clothes closet—right where the house rules said they belonged. We *were* staying with my grandmother!

Morning found us up early and out to the breakfast room by 7:45. The door to the kitchen was open, and a new person worked hurriedly inside. Our hostess came out and scolded us for being early. The house rules specifically listed eight o'clock as the time for breakfast, because the maid could not get there before seven thirty to put the coffee on and get breakfast ready. She also informed me that if I recalled, her e-mail had specified payment upon arrival, so I had to pay now. I gave her my credit card and was scolded again; her e-mail also specifically stated cash only. This was not my grandmother. My grandmother had been a kind, gentle woman. I revised my theories about her: either she killed her husband, or he stole away in the middle of the night, never to return. From now on, she would be Madame X.

At eight o'clock sharp, a harried maid scurried into the breakfast room and apologetically poured coffee and served bread, orange juice, and yogurt. While we were eating, two other couples came in. They were from Sweden and going home today. We had a pleasant conversation, but had to leave so that I could find a bank machine to get cash for Madame X.

Joyce and I walked to the Rialto. This morning was market day. Just below the bridge and along the Grand Canal, stalls offered abundant produce. Vendors were washing fruits and vegetables and arranging them in attractive displays. Farmers, surrounded by tons of artichokes just like those that grew outside our room at Montelucci, were cutting out the hearts and putting them in large tubs of water. Huge, lush blackberries and raspberries spilled out of their boxes. Vendors also sold drinks and sandwiches and all sorts of pastries. The place was jammed with locals doing their early morning shopping, bargaining, and negotiating with the farmers. This scene had been repeated in this place for centuries—so near to, but so different from the glitzy booths selling the vast array of tourist junk.

An interesting thing about Venice is the way it is always changing. There is a sense of compression followed by explosion as one walks through the narrow alleys and then suddenly bursts out into the piazzas. These piazzas, or campos, are lined with shops and restaurants and teeming with people. In the early morning, locals are going to work, and shop owners are getting ready to open for business. During the day, shoppers and tour groups cluster around street vendors from Africa and Asia, whose wares are spread out on rugs on the ground. Gondoliers try to persuade people to take a seventy-five euro, twenty-minute ride; beggars are busy with their trade. The beggars, who could be gypsies or near-easterners, kneel with their arms outstretched, hands open, heads bowed, and eyes closed as the crowds swarm past. They are not nearly as aggressive as American street people. Then, by evening, the vendors and beggars are gone, and the piazzas are filled with couples walking arm in arm—window shopping, looking for a place to eat, or just passing time.

But back to our mission: we had to find a money machine. It had become so easy to get money from access machines in Europe that I no longer bothered with getting traveler's checks before a trip. I also got a better rate of exchange by making withdrawals from my account at the machines, and I didn't have to worry about carrying large sums of money. As we crossed over the Rialto, we emerged into Campo Bartolomeo, a lively square loaded with street vendors and upscale shops selling everything from glass and lace to designer clothing. Joyce immediately came to life. "I'll just wander around here a little while you get the money."

I found a machine, but it would not take my card. I caught Joyce's eye and pointed to a bank. "I'm going to run in there for the money. I'll just be a minute." Italian banks have very tight security. They have revolving doors with a sort of traffic light at them. The doors are locked, and you cannot enter unless the light is green. If someone is leaving, the light stays red until that person is out and the door is completely closed. In some cases, the door will not open if there are too many people inside until someone leaves. And there is always an armed guard inside.

I entered, and there were only two people in front of me. I was about to receive another lesson in the differences of our cultures. Fifteen minutes later, the two in front of me finished their business, and it was my turn—only so I could be told by the teller that their computer was down indefinitely, and I would have to use another bank. I wondered what the two in front of me had been doing all that time. Exiting, I encountered a worried Joyce who wanted to know if there was a problem. Why had I taken so long? I told her I had to find another bank. The same thing happened at the next bank. A little farther on, I found a machine on the street that was from a different bank. It would not take my card either. I was beginning to panic. How was I going to get money? Had something changed since my last trip to Europe? Was I doing something wrong?

Finally, I found a machine that worked. I loved this machine; I would use it often. We hurried back to pay our room bill. Upon entering the second floor, I was greeted by Madame X, who sternly told me the house rules specifically said we were not to return during this time period, because the maid should clean our room undisturbed. I politely informed her that I was only returning to pay my bill and would not go into my room. She told me I could have waited until the designated return time, and she would not have been worried. That came as a big relief to me. I paid her, received her thanks and a receipt, and left.

Back outside, our destination was St. Mark's Square. On the way, we came upon the most charming little *osteria*: the Tratoria al Nono Ristoro. It was on a side canal and had an outside stone courtyard that opened onto a quiet little canal through ancient-looking iron gates. Murals were painted on one wall, and three gigantic vines (which, we were told, were over one hundred years old) trellised over our heads, covering the entire courtyard. We had to stop for lunch; it was too quiet, serene, and romantic to pass without stopping. Of course, the food and wine were excellent. Then we were able to continue to St. Mark's.

A little farther along the way, in the maze of little alleys that wove around the square, we came upon an artists' coop—an enchanting little shop called Max Art. It was very small, with a low-beamed ceiling, and loaded with dolls, puppets, masks, and other artwork covering every inch of wall and ceiling. We engaged in a delightful conversation with one of the artists and bought one of her hand-carved marionettes as a birthday present for our son Brad. The detail was magnificent, and everything in the store was made by local artisans. So many of the souvenirs in the shops of Venice are cheap imitations made in the far east, it is special to find one of the few authentic mask or marionette makers that are left in the city.

When at last we walked out into St. Mark's Square, we felt the greatest rush of adrenaline from being shot out of that tiny little alley into this grand and dramatic space. The square was vast, and straight across from us was the blinding brilliance of the mosaic-adorned basilica. Thousands of pigeons would land, then flutter off in all directions. There was the constant buzz of hundreds of people who didn't even crowd this grand square, the swell of string ensembles competing with each other at the cafés lining the square, and the heavy gong of the cathedral chimes. The vision was too much to take in all at once; it could pull tears to the most hardened cheeks.

We walked around the square, soaking it all in: the music, the artists, people feeding the pigeons, shops, people eating gelato. We joined the latter, enjoying our own servings of delicious gelato. Then we went into the basilica, different from any other church in Europe. It is a mixture of Asian and Eastern European, and even Gothic, but basically follows the Byzantine style, with five mosquelike domes. The Venetians brought artifacts, icons, and treasures back from their world travels, and those are displayed here. Upon entering, after our eyes adjusted to the darkness, we were entranced by the mosaic floors that are buckled from the water that sometimes enters at high tide or during storms. The gold of the mosaic domes also caught our eye. But the masterpiece of it all, behind the high altar, was the Pala d'Oro, a golden altar screen set with emeralds, sapphires, garnets, amethysts, pearls, rubies, and pieces of topaz. There was just too much to recount. We went up the stairs in the atrium to see the original Triumphal Quadriga, the fourth-century bronze horses taken from Constantinople during the crusades in 1204. They had been moved inside to protect them from deterioration by the weather, and copies are now outside, just like Michelangelo's *David* in Florence.

We went outside on the walkway around the domes to enjoy the fabulous view of the square and the islands beyond, then went on to tour the Doge's Palace and the Bridge of Sighs.

Back out in the square, we were told Mel Gibson was shooting a new movie, *Casanova*, in St. Mark's Square every morning. The city authorities required they finish shooting by 10:00 AM in order to open the square to the tourists. We thought we'd like to see a movie being made, but we already had big plans for the next day; it would be Tuesday, the day we were to visit the shrine of St. Anthony in Padua.

That evening, we changed into nicer clothes and walked back across the Rialto to a delightful café, Tratoria Da Gianni, on Strada Nuova behind the Ca D'Oro, which we had enjoyed visiting on our last trip to Venice. We took a table out on the *strada* and had a great meal while being serenaded—first by an accordion player, and later, by two men playing a sax and violin. We had scallops, veal in wine sauce, and tiramisu with water and wine for 47.85 euros. From the next table, a couple made conversation with us. They were from Hampton, Virginia; he had retired from real estate, and this was their first trip to Europe. He knew of Joyce's cousin, who also lived in Hampton, and promised to call him when he got home to tell him of our meeting.

It was a beautiful evening with a full moon, so we strolled the area on our way home. Venice is a very romantic city, but at the same time, we could sense the mystery in the narrow alleys and bridges over little canals. It was very dark and a bit spooky, yet there were lovers strolling arm in arm, and street performers, and charming little courtyards or notches where we could stop and look out over the water. Even though it was late, plenty of people window shopped, strolled, or just lingered. It was truly a wonderful feeling to get into this mode with everyone else. In fact, the Italians have a great expression for it: *il dolce far niente*, the sweet doing nothing. And they do it so well, it becomes contagious.

The next morning, we enjoyed breakfast at 8:15, and then we were off, walking to the train station. We bought round-trip tickets to Padua for ten euros and were there in no time. From the train station, we walked to the Civic Museum and bought tickets to see the Scrovegni Chapel. This tiny chapel is covered from ceiling to floor with a cycle of thirty-eight frescoes by Giotto. The paintings, which depict the lives of Jesus and Mary, are his best work—larger and better preserved than his later work done in Assisi. These brilliantly colored frescoes are considered among the most important early Renaissance art. Great care has been taken to keep them from fading or suffering any other form of deterioration. Therefore, only twenty-five people at a time are allowed inside the chapel for a fifteen-minute visit. The time of our tour was printed on our tickets. If we were late, we would not be permitted in, but would have to purchase new tickets with a new time. Fortunately, we had only an hour to wait for our tour. During peak tourist season, calling ahead to order tickets is suggested, because on the day of the planned visit, all time slots may be filled. In fact, all time slots are often filled days in advance. We were very lucky.

Precisely at our marked time, doors to a sealed glass room were opened, and we were led in to sit and watch a fifteen-minute video about the chapel. While watching the film, our bodies and clothing were being ionized through a special process to clean them of all pollutants, while the previous group was inside the chapel. As the film ended, our door opened to let us in. All backpacks, packages, and cameras had to be left in the passageway to the chapel. Our fifteen-minute visit was worth the wait and all the steps to get in. It was amazing how vibrant the colors were after seven centuries and how real the detail was.

After the chapel visit, we navigated a maze of arcaded streets—built very much under the Austrian influence—to the Piazza del Santo and the very Byzantine-looking Basilica of St. Anthony. The vast expanse of the nave was stunning. We followed the guide booklet to the Treasury Chapel, where the jaw, tongue, and voice box of St. Anthony, all intact, were displayed. Also in this chapel were his original coffin, robe, and the cloth in which his body had been wrapped until his placement in the present tomb.

The tomb's walls were lined with marble reliefs depicting Anthony's life, and the tomb was flanked by two massive seventeenth-century silver candelabra on marble bases. Pilgrims would walk around the tomb; once at the back, they would place their hands on it and pray. We did this, and it was a very spiritual experience. It was moving to pray there, but even more moving to see all those people of powerful faith filing through. There were people of all ages and conditions of health: a teenaged boy on crutches; an old woman, deep in prayer, struggling to pull herself up from her wheelchair, so that she could stand while touching the grave; some softly weeping; others placing flowers or leaving photos of loved ones. There was a large container for people to leave prayer requests, and there were photos and artifacts from people who had been healed after visiting.

At the Chapel of Benedictions, a friar gave us a private blessing. The experience was so calming, it was difficult to leave. When we finally did, we walked to the Piazza da Frata, where market day was in progress, then on to Café Pedrocchi—known for being the in place where famous political and literary characters have hung out since 1831, when it was built. Henry Beyle, aka Stendhal, had written that it was "the best Italian café, almost as good as the Parisian cafés." After seeing the university—Italy's second oldest, where Galileo taught and Dante was a student—we walked back to the station for our train to Venice.

At the end of our stay in Italy, we were to fly home from Venice on a 6:00 AM flight. In my research, I found the airport had no hotel. I was concerned that a flight that early in the morning would make getting from Venice to the airport in time problematic. I didn't want to stay out on the road, because we would have turned in our rental car and would have no means of transportation. I also did not want to chance waiting until our return to Venice to get a room. When we got off the train from Padua, we went to the tourist information office in the station for help with our arrangements.

I found there would be a 4:30 AM bus leaving the Piazzelle Roma that would get us to the airport by five. They assured me we would have no problem getting a room close to the Piazzelle. We moved over to the hotel-reservation station to book a room. Venice was very crowded, and I wanted to be sure we had a decent place confirmed that was within walking distance. The places between the station and the Piazzelle looked seedy, and the neighborhood didn't seem safe for pre-dawn walking. I didn't want to be worrying about this through the rest of our trip.

We booked a room that looked decent enough. It was rather expensive, but I felt it was worth the money to calm my fears. After we booked it, Joyce and I walked to the hotel to gauge the distance. It turned out to be farther than we thought. We would have to walk over three bridges carrying all of our luggage—and then back over those three bridges at four in the morning. I was feeling uneasy about this—a middle-aged couple carrying baggage through deserted streets at 4:00 AM. We would be easy targets for thieves, rapists, and murderers, but I kept these thoughts to myself. Joyce voiced concern, but I assured her that there was nothing to worry about.

That evening, we walked to The Jazz Bar by the Rialto Bridge and had a Bellini. We had to have one; they are a delightful mixture of peach nectar and prosecco and were created at the famous Harry's Bar in Venice. We never ventured into Harry's for the originals, thinking they would have been too expensive. We need not have worried; these imitations cost us twelve euros each. How much more could the originals possibly have been?

Near the bar was an interesting and disturbing site. We were walking along the Salizzada San Giovanni Crisostamo, past the church of the same name. The stones had been pulled up, with wooden walkways laid in their place. Some type of restoration work was going on. We decided to go into the church. As we walked over the little wooden bridge that had been erected to gain entrance, I looked down and noticed there had once been four stone steps to climb for entry into the church. We were now walking directly at street level into it; the stone steps were below us. The church had sunk that much. I don't know what the restoration work exactly was, but I hoped beyond hope that they would be able to stop this sinking that was even more evident than the sight of St. Mark's Square underwater at high tide.

The next day, up at six in the morning and heading to St. Mark's Square, we were excited to see Mel Gibson making his film. The stradas and calles were filled with locals going to work and merchants getting their stores ready for the day's business. It was a pleasantly cool morning.

When we got there, the square was filled with actors and crew shooting a mob scene. All these people were to run through the square on cue, chasing a horse-drawn carriage, shouting, and brandishing farm implements. Of course, Mel was not in this scene; he was not in any scene. It wasn't until we returned to the States that we found Mel had nothing at all to do with this movie. How do rumors get started? At any rate, they shot the mob scene, with no one we recognized, over and over for what seemed like an eternity, until we finally left. Of course, back in the States, when the movie was released, it was interesting to see that scene and realize the people we didn't recognize were the main characters in the movie and very popular. We hadn't realized how out of touch we were, but it was interesting to watch a film being made. I learned how terribly boring it is to be an actor. Doing the same thirty-second scene over and over; enduring the long wait between takes while groups of seemingly unorganized people all talked at the same time about it; and then repeating the take again and again—it's not for the impatient. Those not in the current scene would sit and drink coffee, eat, and play bad jokes on each other out of boredom until it was their turn to do their scene over and over.

Arriving back at the hotel in time for breakfast, we were joined by two other couples—one from British Columbia and another from the Netherlands. The couple from British Columbia was leaving the next day for Greece. They were using Rick Steve's book and had bought his backpacks for the trip.

After breakfast, we said our good-byes and left for Mestre. We got our car out of the garage for fifteen euros (which helped ease the pain of the twenty-four-euro Bellinis), and, as Willie Nelson would say, we were on the road again. We would ride back over the dramatic changes in scenery we had covered four days earlier to Tuscany, then off the Autostrada onto country roads to San Gimignano. Our original plan had also included Volterra for the Etruscan ruins, but there just wasn't enough time. So it would be San Gimignano and then Siena for the night.

Towers, Beautiful Art, and a Severed Head

You know San Gimignano. You see pictures of it all the time. It is the most pop-ular of all Tuscan hill towns, the day trippers' delight. It's called "the medieval Manhattan" because of all the towers—at one time, there were seventy-four of them. Today, there are fourteen. These towers had been built in the thirteenth century as defenses against warring families. They became status symbols; the wealthier the family, the higher the tower. This practice apparently reached its zenith in San Gimignano, which is why crushing hordes of photo-taking, souve-nir-buying tourists stampede through what I am certain had once been a quiet lit-tle pastoral hamlet.

From a distance, the view of the town was spectacular, and it seemed quite intriguing. The town really was charming—the perfect picture of a medieval hill town if you could get by the honky-tonk of shops, cheap souvenirs, wine shops, and tour groups crowding through the streets. Tourism overload certainly has had a negative effect on the residents of this little village on a hill, because the workers at the attractions were the rudest, most blasé we encountered on our entire trip. Perhaps they were not to blame. Those tour groups could get pretty ugly.

We had to park in a pay lot outside the town walls for two euros an hour, or twenty euros for the day. That was becoming the magic amount for parking throughout Italy. The streets inside the walls were pedestrian only because they were narrow and the crowds were huge—even at the end of September, when the crowds were supposed to have been thinning. We walked up the main thorough-fare, Via San Giovanni, which led us to the center of town. The area was formed by two interlocking piazzas: Piazza della Cisterna and Piazza del Doumo.

At Piazza del Doumo, we paid six euros each to enter the cathedral, which had changed its name to Collegiata because there was no longer a bishop in residence. As proof of how jaded this town had become, this was the only church in Italy we had to pay to enter, and it was the least interesting. We walked through this very uninspiring place and went on to the Museo Civico and Torre Grossa, where we had to pay another five euros each to enter.

The museum housed some uninteresting art and sat at the base of the largest tower in town. The entrance, gift shop, and halls were filthy. Signs in English instructed us not to take photos, not to touch the art, not to take water into the museum, and to check all belongings in the lockers (conveniently located in the back of the gift shop). However, once inside the museum, signs at all the works of art were in Italian only—and, miraculously, none of the workers spoke English. Apparently, in their eyes, Americans were the only tourists who needed to be told in their own language not to touch the artwork and how to act, but also didn't have enough interest in culture to be given information about the works of art. We felt insulted and totally ripped off.

But we had already paid, so we decided to hike up the 221 steps to the top of the tower. The view of town, the other towers, and the surrounding Tuscan countryside was well worth the money and the climb. Back down on the ground, Joyce went to find a restroom, where she had to wait in line for a toilet that was tiny and filthy and consisted of a small hole in the floor with depressions on each side for the feet. She paid one euro for the privilege.

We decided to be forgiving and walked to the Piazza della Cisterna. It was ringed with souvenir shops and shops selling Tuscan pottery for the price of a nice-sized house in the United States. The area was also loaded with day trippers. We decided to sit at an outside table at Le Terraze, which is located in front of the Hotel La Cisterna, for a glass of wine and some people watching. A small plaque identified this place as a setting in the film *Tea with Mussolini*, and we are suckers for places that were used in movies. The crowd watching was pleasant enough, but we really didn't like this town, and it was time to move on to Siena. We wanted to get there, find a room before dark, and then have a leisurely meal, perhaps taking part in the *passeggiata*. It didn't happen that way.

These two towns are not far apart; we thought it would be a quick drive. About six kilometers outside of town, we passed a charming-looking inn and restaurant housed on a farm. It was part of the agrotourism business of Italy, similar to the Montelucci. It could have been pleasant, but it was on a small piece of land, and the surrounding area was very industrial and unattractive. The Montelucci had spoiled us. We were close enough to Siena to wait and get something a little better in town.

I had pictured Siena as a small hill town. It was not. It was actually a city of sixty thousand people, which I should have known from all the research I had done, and there was no view of it from a distance. The last six kilometers were industrial and city sprawl: congested, unattractive, and jammed with traffic. As we entered the town proper, small hotels and inns appeared. We stopped at one on a busy street with no parking. I had to park around the corner and was running to the front door when I noticed a sign on the door: *Tutti Occupato*. We were to become very familiar with that sign; everything in Siena was *tutti occupato*.

Finally, as it was getting dark, we came upon a visitor-information kiosk. After finding a parking space four blocks away, we walked to it. It was a hotel cooperative. A couple stood in front of us, and two more stepped in line behind. When our turn finally came, the man inside told us that everything in Siena was sold out. However, he did have a very charming place that still had one room available. It was called Hotel Anna. The three-star hotel was located just three kilometers from where we were and cost 125 euros for the night, including breakfast. It was more than we wanted to pay, but it was late, we were tired and hungry, and if we didn't take it, the people behind us would. And after all, it was three stars, which in Europe pretty much assured a good place. We took it, paid a deposit to him, and left to find it.

Hotel Anna happened to be three kilometers back on the same road we had just traveled. We had passed the nondescript building on this busy road without noticing. We checked in, had to leave our passports at the desk, and were given our key. Upon opening the door to our room, we were almost knocked over by the smell. It smelled as though they had been using this room to store dead animals. The floor was linoleum and sticky. In an effort to air out the room, I opened a window to deafening traffic noise, then went into an even worse-smelling bathroom to open that window. For the first time on our trip, Joyce turned to me and with firm resolve said, "I can't stay here."

I said, "Don't touch a thing. I'll be right back." Knowing there was nothing left in town, I went down to the desk and told the man the room was unacceptable—it smelled and was noisy. Could we have a room that did not smell, and one that was in the back, where it would be quieter?

He changed our room. This one smelled, but the smell was of disinfectant, the floor was not sticky, and the room was in the back. I opened our window, which overlooked the car lot and our car. The view was ugly, but the room was quiet. We left everything in the suitcases, put them on tables in case there were little friends crawling around on the floor, and went out to find food. The street was too busy to walk along, and nothing was open except a tiny restaurant inside the building next to ours. The name was Menu, which made me feel a little suspicious. If they couldn't be any more creative on the name, what would the food be like?

We went in. It was a very small room with ten tables. The owner was greeter, waiter, and cook. Interestingly, the Menu had no printed menu. Selections were offered verbally, and in Italian only. The owner/waiter/chef spoke no English but was extremely flowery in presenting the choices for the evening. There were three men at the table next to ours: two Canadians and an Austrian. We found they had been in the military and met in Italy during the Second World War. They were now meeting back in Italy as a reunion and having a great time. But as we were waiting for our food, we couldn't help hearing them complain about their hotel—it was the Anna. Two more couples came in as we were eating. They were the two couples who had been behind us at the kiosk, and they had been assigned to the Anna. One couple was Italian, the other from Philadelphia. We all had a good laugh over the enterprise of this guy at the kiosk and his Anna partners and the fact that everyone in this savvy group of travelers had been duped into getting the "last" room at the Anna. It turned out to be a very pleasant evening of camaraderie and superb food.

By the time the evening was over, we were exchanging e-mail addresses and singing songs. The owner had given everyone complimentary bruschetta and was leading the singing. The Philadelphia couple promised to look up my old college roommate who now lived in Philadelphia, and the Austrian was kissing Joyce's hand. We returned to the Anna, bellies full, feeling better about our night ahead. We managed a relatively good night's sleep. At least the bed linens were clean and no little friends bothered us, but the shower stall seemed a little scary.

In the morning, after a breakfast about as good as the room, we promptly checked out and returned to the historic part of Siena, a city of the Middle Ages. The neighborhoods of Siena are very hilly and clustered along three ridges that form a kind of wishbone. It is possible to walk along busy pedestrian-only streets loaded with shops that ride the ridges, or to cross down and up very steep hills to get from one ridge to the other. We parked on a street lined with meters right outside the fortress walls that define the historic center, paying a bargain rate of one euro per hour.

Directly in front of us and across a deep gorge, rising out of a mass of tightly clustered brick buildings, was the imposing twelfth-century black-and-white-striped marble Duomo Santa Maria dell Assunta, truly one of Italy's most beautiful Gothic churches. While the building was straight ahead and an impressive photo op, it was a twenty-minute walk away because of the topography. The walk was delightful as we ambled through the perfectly preserved medieval cobbled streets.

Once at the cathedral, we spied a sign telling us we had to wait forty-five minutes for it to open. Standing in the massive square fronting it, we noticed an interesting structure across from the entrance. We walked over to discover the ornate and most beautifully frescoed Ospedale di Santa Maria della Scala, which had been an active hospital from 800 to 1990. The building was now being used as a museum, and the fifteenth-century frescoes were magnificent.

Back across the square, a line had formed for the cathedral. We joined in the line right behind our gentlemen friends from Menu and picked up conversation from the night before. Upon entering the cathedral, we were awestruck by the explosion of color and ornamentation. The columns continued the black and white marble stripes of the exterior, the ceilings were covered with tiles of multiple colors, and the floors were a crazy quilt of fifty-six etched and inlaid marble panels that had been created by forty artisans. These panels, depicting both biblical and mythological subjects, were roped off; most of the year, they are covered with plywood to keep them preserved. Fortunately for us, they are uncovered from September through October, at which time a 1.2 euro fee is charged to enter. I guess this was the second church to charge an entry fee, but they only charge when the floors are uncovered, and the sight is well worth the fee. It was a treat to be there at the only time these fantastic works of art could be viewed.

As we were walking down one of the narrow streets to the Piazza del Campo, it started to rain. The stones became very slippery and difficult to negotiate, but eventually, we emerged through a deep archway into a massive, fan-shaped piazza—Siena's main square and the site of the most famous festival in all of Italy. The Palio delle Contrade, held twice a year, can be traced back to 1310. It is a colorful pageant in which members of each *contrada*, or neighborhood, dress in medieval costumes representative of their group. The whole affair culminates with a horse race in the square, which has been covered with dirt. The *contrada* to win the race gets to keep a beautifully embroidered cloth, which is actually the *palio*. Thousands flock to Siena each July and August to take part in this spectacle. Today, the campo, which was laid out in the twelfth century on the site of a Roman forum, was not covered with dirt. Its herringbone bricks were slippery and covered with hundreds of tour groups, each leader brandishing an umbrella or flag to keep their flock in tow.

The massive early fourteenth-century Palazzo Publico, or city hall, dominated the square. A crenellated gothic building adorned with the fourteenth-century, 337-foot-tall Torre di Mangia, houses the Museo Civico, home of a great collection of Sienese art. This time, we chose not to climb the 503 steps to the top of the tower. It was unfortunate that tourist-trap gift shops and eateries now dominated to the detriment of an otherwise beautifully designed center that, in times before tourist blight, would have been the place to be and be seen. But we had seen enough. Perhaps after the hordes of day trippers left, it might be nice … but then again, we were day trippers too.

On the way out of the Campo, we met the Italian couple from the Anna in front of the Fonte Gaia, a reproduction of Jacapo della Quercia's fourteenth-century fountain. We took a picture of them with their camera, and they took a picture of us with our camera; then we exchanged a few pleasantries before departing.

Walking back to the car along one of the crowded, shop-lined streets, we stopped to buy a watercolor of the Tuscan countryside and some very different yarn from which Joyce would knit a scarf. We also stopped at the Church of San Domenico, which houses the Chapel of Saint Catherine of Siena. In it we were able to view, of all things, her severed head in a gilded tabernacle. It seems St. Catherine died in Rome on April 29, 1380 and was buried there in a poorly sealed grave. In 1383, her body was moved to the Basilica of Holy Mary above Minevra, also in Rome. Deterioration had caused the head to come apart from the body, so the spiritual director, Raymond of Capua secretly had the head sent to her birthplace, Siena, where it remains today.

On that sobering note, we left Siena for Deruta, home to thousands of factories of all sizes that make the famous Italian pottery—none of which, we hoped, contained severed heads.

Umbria, Sacred Assisi, and Tons of Pottery

As in most Italian towns we visited, Deruta had the modern town—in this case, chock-full of pottery factories and shops—down in the flatland, and the medieval, or historic, town center on the hilltop. Actually, if you are not interested in pottery, Deruta would not be worth the time needed for a visit. The historic section is fairly uninspiring. We wound around the historic center through the characteristic, narrow, barely drivable streets. There were more pottery shops and a few restaurants, but nothing that looked like lodging. Not wanting to get stuck, as we had the night before, we decided to find our hotel first, then case the town.

Back down in the flats near the highway, we came upon a very modern, almost American-looking hotel. Although we had vowed not to stay in anything American-looking in order to get that true Italian experience, the previous night's memory was too fresh. The name of the hotel was Melody, which seemed a bit suspicious after Anna, but we went in and asked to see the room. It was nice and modern and clean, with a minibar and safe; it came with breakfast for just seventy euros. We snapped it up before anyone else could. I figured it probably was built for the throngs of American buyers who traveled there to buy all the pottery we see from Deruta in Williams-Sonoma and all the trendy gift shops in the United States. But that was OK.

We deposited our luggage and went out to explore the street of shops, which started at our door and ran a good two miles. Joyce was afraid we would not have enough time to hit them all before they began to close. I was afraid we would have too much time! We decided to do this in a very orderly manner. We would start at one end, going up one side of the street to the very opposite end of town, then come down the other side. Joyce was fine with this plan, with one condition: "There are two places we have to find," said Joyce as she unfurled a sheet of notepaper she had carried from home. "Williams-Sonoma has a ton of stuff from Grazia Maioliche, and this one—Maioliche F.LLI Calzuola, which was written up in Southern Living." Thus armed, we started our hunt.

I must admit the pottery industry in Deruta was fascinating. These shops exist side by side in what must be a very competitive, but lucrative, market. Large, factory-like places with showrooms in front sat next to small shops with a family member sitting right there in the shop, painting or glazing a piece. In those shops, the artist would stop to wait on us as we entered, always with a cheerful "*Boun journo.*" The two potteries Joyce wanted to see turned out to be the large factory type. In addition to a showroom or two, they had museums of patterns and designs going back generations and even centuries, including family patterns and regional patterns. They all had a history, which gave meaning to these patterns I had seen but never thought much about.

Alas, we had hit the two must-sees and several more, yet found nothing we wanted to purchase, when time ran out. The shops closed for the day, and it was time for my favorite activity: dinner. I still had not become accustomed to the late dining in Italy. We didn't participate in this lateness by choice, but rather the fact that the restaurants didn't open until seven. We found we were usually the first into a restaurant as it was opening, and would be finishing our meal as people started to arrive.

A little before seven, we were cruising the streets and alleyways, looking for any place that might be open. We came upon a little hole in the wall sporting a sign: Osteria Il Borghetta. The door was standing open. Hesitantly, we approached. Inside, a man and woman were seated at one of about eight empty tables. When we asked if they were open, they jumped up and insisted we take their seats. With a grand gesture, the man introduced himself as Filberto Guttuso, the owner, and his wife as the cook. Then he said something to her in Italian that probably meant, "Fire up the oven—we have two live ones!" She quickly disappeared into the kitchen as he handed us the menu and proceeded to read the whole thing to us, translating it into English, with full and artful descriptions of each dish.

They made everything themselves, delivered each dish to the table, and stood over us as we ate, asking how we liked each bite. The woman spoke no English and didn't say a word, but smiled broadly every time we told her in our fractured Italian that something tasted good. "*Bouno!*"—smile. "*Molto bouno!*"—smile. "*Tuti molti bouno!*"—bigger smile.

The man spoke throughout the meal, asking about us and our visit, and telling us his story. Born in Sicily, he had traveled all over Italy, bartended in Venice, married, and then decided to move to his wife's parents' village outside of Deruta and open this restaurant.

The food was fantastic: a huge platter of prosciutto, beautifully arranged with pecorino in the middle and garnished with chopped nuts and basil; gnocchi topped with three cheeses, including brie; a bowl of melt-in-your-mouth beef stew served with polenta, which had fava beans resting in a well in the middle; roasted potatoes and salad; and of course, a bottle of wine and water. All this for thirty-seven euros? While I was terribly pleased—and stuffed—I did worry that he would soon be out of business.

At the end of the meal, he gave each of us a spoon and brought out a bottle of balsamic vinegar from Modena that had been aged twenty years. He delicately poured a little into each spoon and asked us to drink. It was thick as syrup, very dark, and deliciously sweet. He told us it was a very expensive delicacy that was to be drunk like this as a digestive.

It was a most pleasant evening. As we were leaving, another couple was entering. We hoped more people would arrive soon. Perhaps the place would fill up later; we were, of course, earlier than any respectable Italian would be. Back at our clean room and totally satiated, we had a great night's sleep.

In the morning, we enjoyed a good breakfast and returned to our quest for the perfect piece of pottery. That road was longer than two miles, and the shops could have continued into the next town, but prudence forced us to stop at the city line and start back down the other side. At the last—and I do mean the very last—shop, Joyce found exactly what she wanted.

Geribi Ceramics was a midsize shop. A thirty-four-year-old woman from New Zealand did some of the painting and glazing, handled all sales, and managed the store. The owner and a few relatives did all the pottery work. Every piece was hand painted. We met another couple in the store. They were from Philadelphia and on their honeymoon. They were buying a set of china and some odd pieces. I remembered our honeymoon; back then, in the day before credit cards, we had driven from Cape Cod, bought a small figurine, and then come up short when trying to pay the turnpike toll to our destination. We had to get off the highway early and take back roads the rest of the way home.

At this late stage in our lives, these young people were outspending us. But not to fear—this time, we had plastic and were holding our own. We bought the kids biscotti jars and one for ourselves, but we didn't stop there. No—we bought our own set of dishes. Because everything was hand painted to order, and I would have needed a U-Haul to take everything with us, we had the order shipped home. We were told the order would arrive by the holidays, and the shipping charge would be by the box—therefore, the same if we **put** one item in or fifty, as long as everything went in one box. So we did our best to load that box to the legal limit. Now we could leave for Assisi.

St. Francis has always been one of my favorites; his **love for** nature and wildlife and his serene life and devotion have always been **an inspiration** to me. I was looking forward to visiting Assisi and his hermitage **in the hills** above. Our son and daughter-in-law visited on their honeymoon and **said it had** been one of their favorite places. They had hiked to Ermeo delle **Carceri, the** hermitage atop Monte Subasio where Francis and his followers retreated to pray and meditate. Finding it peaceful and calming, our son and his wife **had** recommended we do the same.

Assisi came into view as we approached from the valley of fields and olive groves below. It was an impressive sight. Layers of pink and gray stone buildings with tiled roofs sprawling across the mountainside were framed by the massive Basilica di San Francesco on one side, the steeple of Assisi's Duomo on the other, and its castle, Rocca Maggiore, towering above. We had booked a room in the Hotel Umbra, which we had found in Karen Brown's *Italy: Charming Inns & Itineraries*. We had used her guides on other trips and were never disappointed. This would prove to be no exception.

The streets of Assisi were pedestrian only, except for deliveries and passenger unloading. We pulled up to one of the gates of this walled hill town and were greeted by an impeccably dressed policewoman in starched white shirt and pressed blue slacks that sported a broad red stripe down the seam. I showed her my reservation, and she gave brief directions before allowing us to proceed. Inching forward was a bit scary. The streets were only a car width wide, and they were loaded with people walking in complete oblivion to the possibility of ever seeing a car. So we crawled as people slowly moved aside—sometimes after long moments of cluelessness—praying to get to our destination without killing someone.

Our hotel was right off the main square, Piazza del Comune, across from the remarkably well-preserved portico of the first century BC Roman Temple of Minerva and down a fourteenth-century stone alley. Parts of our building were built on top of Roman foundations. The place was charming. We entered through a wooden gate into a lush garden, where breakfast was served in the summer, and then into a cheerful lobby, where we were greeted most graciously by the daughter of the owners.

Up a flight of stairs, our room was large and decorated in the classic Italian style. It had a sitting area, an ornately upholstered headboard, and two sets of shuttered windows that looked out over red-tiled rooftops, the Basilica Santa Clara, and Duomo San Ruffino, where St. Clara and St. Francis had been baptized. We could also see the mountain beyond, where St. Francis had made his hermitage. To complement this fabulous view, the chimes of the two churches would softly toll on the hour.

Outside our door and a few steps toward the back of the building was a door that led onto a rooftop terrace with a breathtaking view of the town below, along with the broad Spoleto Valley and mountain range beyond. That would become the place where Joyce and I would have our evening predinner wine, write in our journals, and sink into relaxed ecstasy as we listened to all the churches in town chime the evening Angelus.

After checking in, unpacking the car, moving it to a pay lot outside the walls, and walking back to the hotel, we went to a bar in the square for something to eat. The main square was ringed with restaurants, wine bars, and shops. The end opposite the gleaming white pillars of Minerva showcased an impressive multit-iered fountain at the apex of a burst of streets lined with trendy clothing stores, tacky souvenir and religious-article shops, and homes. St. Francis had grown up in a house on one of those side streets. The whole town was a living museum.

We decided to explore the town, working our way toward the massive Basilica di San Francesco. This most visited shrine, or pilgrimage site, after Rome and Bethlehem anchored the western end of town and provided a commanding view over the entire valley. There we toured the upper and lower basilicas. The upper basilica had been badly damaged in the earthquake of 1997, when over two tons of debris, including some priceless 700-year-old frescoes, crashed down from the vaulted ceilings. As devastating as this was, it was fortunate the famous frescoes by Giotto of the life of St. Francis survived. It was impressive to see them, but Giotto's work at the Scrovegni Chapel was, I thought, more spectacular and bet-ter preserved.

It was moving to go under the lower basilica to the tomb where St. Francis and four of his closest followers are buried. From there, we went through a small museum in the building which housed his robe, his sandals, the stone on which he was originally placed before the new tomb was built, and the suede cloth that had covered his stigmata. Time spent here was peaceful and spiritual in spite of the large crowds.

Walking back to the hotel, we stopped at a cybercafé to e-mail the kids and buy a piece of chocolate torrone—a sinful confection that is lavishly displayed in numerous shop windows throughout Italy. Back at the hotel, we had our wine and torrone appetizer out on the rooftop deck. Another couple had the same idea and came out onto the deck for their predinner drink. As we talked, we found they were from California. They loved Italy and Assisi and visited the country every year. They were planning to buy a place on one of the small islands near Venice for their retirement home. We had a delightful conversation, then returned to our room, showered, changed into more formal clothing, and went down to the hotel's beautifully baroque dining hall for an artfully prepared and served gourmet dinner. It was a very pleasant evening.

In the morning, we hiked four kilometers out of town to the hermitage. That doesn't sound far, but it was all uphill, along a rather busy road with no sidewalks in what seemed like a very humid 90 degrees. Our children had taken a footpath from the Rocco Maggiore, but thought it a bit tricky, so we decided to take the road. The farther we went, the steeper the climb seemed. At least we had enough sense to carry bottled water this time. We finally reached the top, totally soaked with perspiration and gasping for air. It was well worth the exertion.

The view was magnificent; we could see the town below and the Spoleto Valley beyond as if we were looking down from an airplane. On the hermitage grounds, a friary, consisting of a cluster of very small rooms and narrow passageways, was irregularly perched on the cliff edge. Beyond and all around was a maze of paths and stairs carved into the side of this rugged hilltop where Francis and his followers had walked, prayed, and meditated. Even now, tourists and pilgrims were slowly walking, reading, and praying in hushed reverence.

We saw the thousand-year-old oak tree growing out of a rock ledge where Francis had sat and preached to the birds. It was trussed with iron rods, but still there. We walked the paths, climbed the stairs that had been carved into the cliff side, and looked into the caves where Francis and his followers had slept. The tensions of the outside world and fatigue of the hike were washed away, making us feel as though we could stay there forever. But after about an hour, hunger called, and we started our trek down to town and a great lunch at an outdoor café.

After lunch and a tour of the Basilica of St. Clare, we went back to the room for a quick shower and change of clothes, then went to the main basilica for evening mass. The next day, October 3, was the anniversary of St. Francis's death; a festival was going to be in full swing. We, however, would be leaving that day, because no rooms would have been available, and our itinerary left no time for such diversions. Even tonight, as we approached the basilica, the streets outside were filled with TV trucks and the buzz of cameras and platforms being erected. There was also a large crowd outside, and many of the people were, by appearance, high-level clergy in full regalia.

We did manage to get inside, and even to find a seat. The place was jammed. Behind the altar were assembled a massive choir and musicians. Mass began with a procession of eight servers and twenty priests and clerics. There were hundreds of priests and nuns in the crowd, which spilled out into the street. The service and the music moved us to tears. The singing was some of the most beautiful I have ever heard. We felt very fortunate to have been in this spot at this time.

After mass, we walked up one of the highest streets to a restaurant we had spotted earlier. The Ristorante Bar Metastasio held a commanding position. Inside was a charming dining room in what seemed to be an old Roman cellar, made of stone walls with an arched, cavelike ceiling. But because, as usual, we were the first to enter, we snagged the best table, outside on a flower-decked balcony with that fantastic view of the entire region. We sipped wine, watched a glorious pink and purple sunset, ate great food, and soaked in the scenery for a perfectly peaceful and romantic last night in Assisi.

On Sunday morning, the festivities really began. The square outside our hotel slowly filled with people for the procession. I thought we had better get the car in, loaded, and out before officials closed the square off for the day. Walking to the car, I noticed signs were posted on walls around the main square marking where various groups were to gather for the procession. As we were leaving, I spied a sign for Abruzzo, my father's native province, and spotted a bus full of people parked in front of it. I felt as though I were getting closer to my roots.

We just beat the crowds out of town on our way to Spoleto. Once again, we found the streets of Spoleto barely manageable, so we parked at the first spot we found—next to a first century AD Roman amphitheater—and walked into the historic center of town. For years, Joyce and I have wanted to attend the Spoleto festival in Charleston, South Carolina, but haven't. It is a festival of music and the arts that has been co-celebrated in Charleston and Spoleto since 1958. It was founded by composer Gian Carlo Menotti and named Festival dei Due Mondi (Festival of Two Worlds). It was fun to see the banners throughout this sister town advertising what had become a world event celebrated in our own Charleston as well. The festival aside, Spoleto was an intriguing town. A settlement had been on that site as early as the Bronze Age. It was a Roman town by the third century BC and had withstood an attack by Hannibal.

We walked through the Piazza del Mercato and stopped to rest at the third-century fountain that was still treating strollers to its water. Through streets filled with shops, we emerged onto the Piazza del Duomo and the dramatic site of the twelfth-century cathedral, a beautiful setting high up on a hilltop plateau.

After going through the cathedral, we walked on to the Rocca Albornoz, a sturdy, fortresslike place built in 1539 for the papal envoy Cardinal Albornoz. It had temporarily served as the home to Lucrezia Borgia, who I found was the teenage daughter of Pope Alexander VI. Very interesting—daughter of a pope? Hmm … all this debate about celibacy in the priesthood wasn't tackling such a new issue after all. I guess that far back, those guys were living the Nike philosophy and just did it. We then walked across the Ponte delle Torri, a fourteenth-century bridge built on top of a Roman aqueduct. It had a panoramic view of the valley bellow and the Rocca above.

This seemed like an intriguing town, and it would have been nice to spend more time here; alas, we had to get to Orvieto. Once again, we were trying to pack too much in. But we had made room reservations from Assisi at a sister hotel to the Umbra and wanted to get there before evening.

The drive to Orvieto was thrilling. We traveled twisting, turning country mountain roads that careened out over cliffs, down into lush farm valleys, and up again into the sky. At one point, we drove alongside a large lake set deep in a valley of vertical rock and ending at a large dam. The dam was being patrolled by a guard carrying a machine gun. Now these people knew how to do homeland security.

One of the reasons I wanted to see Orvieto was that it was probably one of the most dramatically set hill towns in Italy. Originally Etruscan, it sat atop a thousand-foot-high plateau of volcanic rock in the middle of a wide valley. It had been destroyed and rebuilt in 264 AD by the Romans. As did the Etruscans before them, the Romans sculpted numerous tunnels into the porous tufa butte as storage caves, cisterns, and living spaces. It was possible to take a tour of underground Orvieto. At one time, Orvieto was a prominent papal seat, and over thirty-three popes have had their summer residences there. It was most wellknown for its church, a thirteenth-century gem of art. The façade was brilliantly covered with mosaics and said to become a shimmering spectacle as the sun was setting. Inside the cathedral, in the Chapel of San Brizo, was one of the greatest cycles of the Renaissance: the Last Judgment, began by Fra Angelico and completed by Luca Signorelli.

We were staying at a hotel at the base of the butte, but we chose to drive to the top rather than ride the funicular (cable car) that connected the lower, more modern part of town to the upper, historic section. After parking in the pay lot and walking the adjacent park with views of the countryside below, we maneuvered the crowded narrow streets to the church. Inside, something was about to happen. The place was filling with people, many very well dressed. Ushers were passing out booklets. We went directly to the chapel to find it roped off and filled with all levels of clergy. The usher at the ropes did allow us to enter, and we were able to see the cycle, but did not stay long.

Back in the main part of the church, candles were being lit and tiny lights lining the walls and ceiling around the altar came to life and flickered like candles. A choir began singing. We took a standing space along the wall and waited to see what was happening. Glorious music erupted as a procession of sixty priests, a young man in the middle wearing a white robe and surrounded by nuns carrying candles inside lanterns on top of long metal poles, the young man's family members, and finally two bishops and a cardinal filed out of the chapel. We were witnessing the ordination of the priest in white. The pageantry was spectacular, and the music some of the most moving I ever heard, equaling that of Assisi. But, once again, our stomachs called, and as soon as the procession ended and the service began, we slid out a side door and into the square in pursuit of food.

We chose a café on the square and took a table with a full view of the church façade and the passing crowds. We would have some wine and a pizza and watch the spectacle of the sunset. It was a beautiful setting. The food was terribly expensive and lousy, but we loved the ambience, even though we were getting stiffed in the process. Sunset came and went; the crowds gathered, stared at the church front for a while, and left, but nothing notable happened. So much for the glorious, shimmering facade. We walked back to the car and drove to the hotel. It was such a beautiful place and so expensive we decided to spend the evening enjoying it.

As I said earlier, we liked our hotel in Assisi so much that we had booked this place from there before leaving. Both hotels belonged to a group called (cleverly, I thought) Charme and Relax. At Assisi, we picked up the Charme and Relax booklet that listed, with descriptions in Italian and English and plenty of photos, 164 of their hotels throughout Italy. They were three-or four-star hotels and looked very nice but were rather expensive. The Umbra in Assisi and the Anna were both three stars—go figure. So much for the Italian rating system! It seemed that the cost, rather than the star, was a better predictor. After being stung by the Anna, we chose expensive. Then again, the Anna had hardly been cheap. Something certainly had changed in Italy since our last visit.

The four-star Albergo Villa Ciconia was an elegant sixteenth-century villa nestled in a thick grove of trees on a bend of the Carcione River. The lovely stone structure boasted twenty-foot ceilings and terra-cotta floors. It had a beautiful dining room with a painted, beamed ceiling and massive fireplace. Twelve-foot-high windows overlooked a swimming pool, a grove of fruit trees, and the river, which surrounded the villa on three sides. A grand stone stairway led up to a sitting room; our room beyond mirrored the grandeur of the downstairs, featuring an iron canopied bed, massive armoire, sitting area, and complimentary fruit basket.

We got comfortable, opened the windows and a bottle of Campo di Massi 2003 Umbrian wine, and lounged on our king bed. We ate fruit, read, and wrote in our journals in total silence, except for the slight ruffle of a breeze through the trees and the rippling of the river rolling by our window. Feeling refreshed in the morning, we had the best breakfast on the trip and left for Abruzzo to begin our quest for my roots.

I must note that while we enjoyed our night at Villa Ciconia, we found the staff to be stuffy and reserved to the point of unfriendliness—something we were not to find anywhere else on our trip. I also noticed they displayed an old copy of Karen Brown's book that contained a write-up of their hotel; it was not in our more recent copy. She must have also sensed the same slight hostility.

Finding Relatives and a Father's Childhood in Abruzzo

Now, halfway through our trip and en route to my father's childhood home, I was feeling excited and apprehensive. I wanted to research my family, but what if we turned up nothing? What if my relatives did not want to see us? After all, we never heard from them after my grandfather died. They must not have been interested. If nothing else, I'd get to walk the streets where my father played as a boy and possibly gain access to church records.

Immediately, we took the Autostrada all the way to Sulmona. There is something liberating about a multilane toll highway—very American. It is relaxing to drive without worrying about where to turn. Although I really enjoyed the back roads and magnificent scenery, I had a sense of familiarity on the Autostrada. But the scenery was more dramatic than on the long interstate drives back home. In a short distance, we went from the hills of Umbra through the flatlands around the outskirts of Rome, then zoomed into the towering mountains of Abruzzo.

These highest peaks of the Apennine Range became jagged and green with pine forests, then changed to the arid and rocky brown of Southern Californian mountains. Once again, I marveled at the magnificent feats of Italian engineering: tunnels opened to huge expanses of bridgework, which swung out over gorges, then led back into tunnels and out again.

Exiting the Cocullo tunnel, I lost my breath at the sheer drop. The hilltop towns of Cocullo and Bugnara, of my father's family, and Pacentro, of my mother's father's childhood, occupied the same view at once against a backdrop of the snowcapped Grand Sasso. Suddenly, an elephant lodged in my throat, and my eyes stung. My head was spinning as I tried to absorb everything before it all disappeared from sight.

It was beauty and drama and history—my history. It was geography—my geography. When my father talked of the beautiful hills and streams where he played as a boy, this is what his mind saw—something vastly different than the smoke-choked steel valley where he spent the rest of his life. Maybe that is why he talked so little of this place: the loss was too painful, the difference too severe.

Swooping down from the mountaintops and into the broad valley of Sulmona, we left the Autostrada and drove into the center of town. Sulmona is a delightful town of 25,000 people. It sits in the broad Peligna valley (which makes it flat and uncommon in Italy) surrounded by hilltop villages, medieval fortresses, and the highest mountains of the Apennines. It was the home of the poet Ovid, who was born there in 43 BC. During the Swabian Period, it was the capital of the region.

According to tradition, Sulmona was founded by Solimo Frigio, one of Aenea's companions (who, after fleeing Troy, decided to stay). It is known for its large sheep-raising area, for being a railroad center, for its artisans (notably gold-smithing), and, most recently, for making confetti, the great almond candy provided at Italian weddings. The town was filled with shops selling confetti in every shape and form. It was possible to buy trees and flowers made of confetti, along with wreaths, hats, and other clothing made of this glorious confection.

Sulmona was a hidden jewel, a lovely city. The historic core was walled, and the elaborate gates were in excellent condition. Narrow walking streets were lined with trendy designer shops and small stores selling gold jewelry made by the artisan shop owners. These shops also offered handmade lace and linens—and, of course, confetti. The town even has a *palio* in August, seemingly as impressive as the highly touted *palio* of Siena, yet I had never heard of it. We went directly to the visitor's center, housed on the first floor of the fifteenth-century Palazzo della S.S. Annunziata, now the civic museum. There, we were given information on lodging by a hospitable woman.

We chose the Hotel Italia, a one-star hotel in the center of town. I'll admit the one star frightened me. But the lady at the visitor center assured us we would like it, and she was right. It was old, had no elevator, came without breakfast, and took no credit cards. But it was right off Piazza XX Septembre, a principal square in town that featured a statue of Ovid.

The hotel was located in what had likely been a magnificent palazzo in its day. We ascended a skylighted, stone spiral staircase and walked down a hall with a vaulted ceiling, reminiscent of a medieval castle. Our room was small and simple, but had French doors opening to a balcony overlooking the street. It was furnished in what we in the United States would refer to as time-worn antiques with a charming patina. Oh, and parking on the street was free if we displayed a card from the hotel on the dash. Best of all, the price of the room was fifty-four euros.

After unpacking, we walked to the main square, Piazza Garibaldi, where the Chivalrous Tournament, as they call their *palio*, is held. This square was larger and lovelier than Siena's Campo, yet almost devoid of tourists. At one end was a thirteenth-century aqueduct; at the other end were the baroque monastery of Santa Chiara and the church of San Fillipo. In the middle, a huge fountain was circled by an oval street—possibly a Roman chariot track at one time. The remaining buildings housed shops and restaurants, but looked as though they had been palazzos from varying periods and architectural styles. Behind the buildings and through gaps in buildings, I could see the steep hills, some of which were adorned with villages, and the snowcapped mountains. Everything was pristine and serene.

One side of the square offered restaurants and cafés with outside seating. Some looked rather chic, and others looked touristy or just plain expensive at best. An unassuming little café with six tables out front caught my eye over the other more glitzy eateries. Three people sat at one table, talking with a man who appeared to be the owner. Behind a beaded doorway, a little old lady dressed in black was cooking.

The owner greeted us and gave the menu verbally. We had a half liter of wine, gnocchi topped with Abruzzese ragu, and bread and water for a total of fourteen euros. The people at the other table opened a box of chocolate torrone and sent five pieces to our table for *dolce*. Everyone was gracious and friendly.

Leaving the piazza, I noticed a man sitting at a bench wearing a baseball cap with the name of our local real-estate company on the front. We walked over to him and asked about the cap. He spoke no English, but said he had visited relatives in western Pennsylvania who had given him the cap. We took his picture, intending to send it to the firm with a comment on their far-reaching agency.

At three in the afternoon, Joyce wanted to do some shopping; the stores were reopening after lunch. I thought we should first call Nancy, our soon-to-be interpreter, to let her know we'd arrived and set a time to meet the next day.

Answering the phone in a gruff tone, Nancy shouted, "Where are you? Your cousin Tilde has been here two days waiting for you. She has taken time off from work. I called my cousin in America, and she called your mother, who said you were in Venice. I called the Hotel Santacroce in Sulmona, and they told us you were not registered."

Nancy had told Tilde the wrong day for our arrival and somehow had deduced we would be staying at the most expensive hotel in Sulmona, not a one-star hotel. I told her we were staying at the Italia and asked when she wanted us at Bugnara.

"Now!" she shouted. "We've been waiting for you!"

I hung up and said, "Plans have changed. We must go to Bugnara right now."

Leaving the hotel, I scraped the side of the car on the corner of a building as I was trying to make a right turn at a very tight intersection. It was necessary to back up and make three tries to get around the corner.

Bugnara was only seven kilometers away, but the drive was laden with apprehension. What would I find? I was actually going to meet my cousin, drive the streets my father had played in as a little boy, see the house he lived in, and talk to people who had known him as a child. I wanted to know so much … but now, I didn't know where to begin or how to go about it.

I recalled the days after the war, when Italy was enduring a difficult period of reconstruction. My parents filled packages with cigarettes for my married aunt's husband, along with hard-to-get cosmetics and toiletries for my aunts and cousins. They wrapped the box with cloth, usually from flour or chicken-feed sacks. My mother then sewed the cloth seams shut. Then my father wrapped the package with twine and melted sealing wax over the seams, so it could not be opened in transit. In photos they had sent from the early fifties, the family members were dressed somberly by our standards and looked quite dour.

The sight of Bugnara jolted me back to reality. It was a fifteenth-century village of twelve hundred inhabitants. As were all of the hill towns, it was built on a hillside topped by a *castello*; this one had once belonged to the Mariconda family. The town was clean looking; every building was painted the same cream color with a red-tiled roof, even the church. It looked as though a great deal of restoration had taken place in recent years. The only exception was the *castello*, which was grayer, crumbling, and in need of extensive repair. While many of these hill-town *castellos* were in ruins, they exuded a certain storybook charm. This one seemed to be less picturesque and more fortresslike.

My gracious hosts never told me this story, but after returning home, Nancy's cousin related the undiscussed story of the *castello*. At one time (she never specified exactly when, but it would have been during the Feudal Period), the *castello* was occupied by the *barone pazzo* (crazy baron). He wore flowing robes and made the townspeople kneel and kiss his ring as he passed. More bizarre was the practice of requiring each engaged virgin in town to spend the night before her wedding with him. He proclaimed this was his right as lord of the town. The standing story related that many families' firstborn children never resembled the rest of their family members, but they all looked very much alike. After doing research, I learned this was a common practice in many medieval villages under the Feudal System. But I could understand why my hosts did not care to share this bit of trivia.

We drove into the center of the little village and parked in the main square, next to the St. Rosario Church. Nancy and Tilde walked to the car before I could get out. My first reaction upon seeing Tilde was surprise. Contrary to the vision in my head all these years, Tilde was attractive and looked quite cosmopolitan. Shorter than Joyce, who was five foot three, Tilde was tiny in stature, fair, and blond. She sported a stylish haircut and wore a chic brown and black knit pantsuit, a gold necklace, and a lovely wristwatch with diamonds. She carried a Louis Vitton handbag. A most pleasant smile revealed straight, white, capped teeth. I detected a keen resemblance to my father.

She embraced Joyce and me and kissed us on both cheeks, inviting us into her house. Nancy, a larger, more robustly built person with a darker complexion, powerful handshake, and commanding voice, greeted us with a smile that could melt butter. Nancy's house was right on the square adjacent to the church, and Tilde's was down a flight of stairs directly behind it.

The house was a handsome, cream-colored stucco, featuring a beautifully carved wooden double door with a rounded top and stone surround. We walked through a living room on spotless, shining tile floors into a heavily furnished dining room centered by a large iron-and-crystal chandelier. The buffet held ornately framed family photos.

Down three steps and through a modernly outfitted kitchen with a tiled fireplace in the corner, she walked us into what had been her parents' bedroom. The room was furnished with exquisite antique-quality walnut furniture. She showed us prominently displayed pictures of my father, taken in the thirties, and wedding pictures of my uncle and my parents. Then she showed us the high school and college graduation pictures I had signed and sent to my grandfather.

Back in the kitchen, we sat around a large table that dominated the center of the room. Tilde quickly put out a dish of pizza pieces, several types of cookies, and little bottles of fruit juices. With Nancy interpreting, we started with pleasantries, and then moved on to my questions.

I got nowhere. Tilde told me the names of my grandmother's and grandfather's parents. She didn't know their birth or death dates. She could tell me nothing further back. She and Nancy looked at us with amusement. Why would we need such useless information? If one were from a wealthy or titled family, this would be important information, but not in our case. We knew three generations back. Why would we need to know more?

Nancy explained, "In Italy, we only look back three generations. That's all."

I was to find through the day that Nancy was direct and succinct in her answers. I'm also not certain her interpretations were accurate, but that's something I will never know, given my command of the language.

From our conversation, I gathered that Italians were amused by the Americans' need to trace their histories. Having lived in this one village for centuries, their sense of place was secure. Why would they question who they were or from where they came? They came from the very town in which they were living. Their homes were hundreds of years old; relatives, friends and neighbors had been around them since time began. What else was there to know? The Italians also knew the future was fragile. They had lived through wars fought right in their towns, in their homes. They had developed a totally different perspective on life.

These people lived in the moment, not wasting time lamenting the past or worrying about the future.

I wasn't going to get much more from them. It seemed this was not the house my father had lived in. His house had been directly behind this one but was so badly damaged in an earthquake that it had to be torn down. This was the house of Tilde's parents, my aunt, and my uncle. My grandfather had lived here with them when he returned to Italy, as had my other aunt. Now that they all were gone, Tilde, living and working near Rome, used it as a weekend home. She was an unmarried math teacher still working at the age of sixty-nine.

She asked all about our family—my mother and aunt, my brother and sister, and our cousins and children. We were both trying to collect as much information as we could—though I wanted the past and she wanted the present. I was moved by the experience of sitting in this kitchen, talking about our family and our history. It was touching to know that they had kept all our pictures. Listening to Tilde through Nancy's interpretation, we were told her mother had missed her brothers and had kept their memory alive through the years.

Our grandmother, having died at a young age, and our grandfather, living in America, left Louise, Tilde's mother, who was then only fifteen, with the responsibility of raising the rest of the children. My father, only three years younger, must have been a handful from the stories Tilde told. But she told them in the sweetest way, as though they were family legends handed down from previous generations. It seemed her mother had been a kind and loving person with nothing but the warmest feelings toward our family in America—a family Tilde had never met but knew so much about.

I wasn't going to get the names, dates, and documentation I had hoped for, but I was going to get something infinitely more valuable: I was going to form a real-life connection with my family. I put my paper and pencil away and decided to sit back and enjoy this ride, however they had it planned for me.

We left the house and walked to St. Rosario Church in the square. Nancy found someone to unlock it for us. The church had been badly damaged in a 1981 earthquake but was totally restored, largely with funds donated by families from this town who now lived in America. Plain on the outside, the structure was exquisitely baroque on the inside. Looking at the names of donors on plaques attached to the backs of pews, I remembered my childhood and all my father's friends who had spent countless joyful hours at our house. There they were Nolfi, LaMarca, D'Eramo, Conti, Colaluca, and Marchione. All of these names leaped out of the past, bringing a rush of memories. I could recall all these people visiting in each other's homes, laughing and singing and truly enjoying the company of their *paesani*, yet keeping ties to their home village as well. Why had my dad never wanted to keep close ties with his sisters? What had been different about him compared to those other men?

In a glass-enclosed alcove stood the statue of Santa Magno, patron saint of Bugnara. Looking at that statue, I remembered the feast days of my youth in West Aliquippa, the enclave where all the Bugnaraese settled. There would be music by the Sons of Italy band (the same band Henry Mancini had played in as a youth) and food booths—lots of food booths. My favorite was the little waxed-paper envelope of lightly salted Lupini beans. They looked like a yellow lima, and when you bit through the plasticlike skin, they would pop into your mouth, releasing an exquisite taste.

Excitement would mount as the doll dance was performed through the streets before the evening ended with a powerful display of fireworks. The next morning, there would be an Italian mass, followed by a procession through town. The festival officers would carry the St. Magno statue on a platform, stopping occasionally so that people could pin money to it. These memories were from a time long past and of celebration forgotten by many, but here was the real thing: St. Magno, in his church, in his town. The memories caught in my throat, and it was hard to talk.

We walked through town and up the hill to another church. Nancy explained this was the church of Madonna della Neve (Our Lady of the Snow). Although this church was hundreds of years old and believed to have been built on top of a Roman temple, it was the newer church. Now that the town population had dramatically declined, two churches were no longer needed. People of the village used one church in summer and for weddings and the other in winter and for funerals.

Behind Madonna della Neve was the cemetery. All the graves were above-ground and stacked on top of each other in little family mausoleums or crypts. We looked at the LaMarca crypt, where Tilde's father's family was interred. Our aunt Louise was there, because once married, the women became part of the husband's family. But Italian women used their maiden name after their married name to maintain the lineage, which I think is a wonderful tradition.

Next was the Iannessa crypt, which held the family of my grandmother, sharing space with the Gentile crypt. Only my grandfather and unmarried aunt were in this crypt. I asked where my grandmother was, if not here.

Nancy answered, "There was an older cemetery. When this one was built, they moved people from the older one to this one. They could not find your grandmother. She must have been in the house of bones."

I asked, "What's the house of bones?"

Nancy pointed to a stucco building at the edge of the cemetery, which had only one door and one barred window. "That's the house of bones. In Italy, we must pay for keeping up the graves. After thirty years, if no one pays, they take the bones out of the grave, and someone else uses it. They put the old bones in the house of bones. In Italy, is the law."

I was shocked by this bit of news—and that these gentle, loving people thought nothing of this practice. It was another insight into the cultural differences. But I guess they are more practical. Space is limited in Italy, which has been much more tightly populated for many centuries. They could run out of burial space, something we think could never happen in the United States. Right now, Americans don't have to face that grim decision.

The cemetery was beautifully maintained, and the main walkway was lined with cypress trees. Nancy explained, "All cemeteries in Italy are lined with cypress trees. Is the law. If you are driving and see a row of cypress, is a cemetery."

I was getting the hang of Nancy's explanations. Everything "is the law," and the reasons are in stark black or white. No gray existed for this lady. But as I thought about it, this was another profound cultural difference. Everything was straightforward and simple. People were honest and direct. No one worried about political correctness before speaking; they just spoke the truth. How refreshing.

I guess there was a time in our country when everyone agreed on what was right and what was wrong as though it were law. But that time has long past. Now every law is challenged and every publicly made statement is disputed. It's all about, "What makes me feel good is right, and if you have a different opinion, you are wrong." In America, are so many arguments for exceptions, I don't think people can agree on right or wrong anymore.

But here, those basic core values haven't changed. They just say straight out what they think, and no one is offended. No one is suing or demanding an apology. Right is right. Wrong is wrong. Black is black, and white is white.

Nancy explained Tilde felt she was not a good cook and wanted to treat us to dinner at a restaurant. I said we wanted to treat them to dinner, especially since Nancy had set up our meeting, and Tilde had taken off from work. Tilde protested, and Nancy explained it would be a great insult if we insisted on paying. Tilde was our host. She said we could treat her when she visited us in America. Also, Tilde wanted to show us Scano. It was the most noted resort in Abruzzo, and no one should visit without seeing it.

As we returned to the car, a young woman, probably around thirty years old, walked toward us. We stopped to talk to her.

After a lengthy conversation, Nancy turned to us and said, "We are all cous- ins. Tilde's father was LaMarca, my mother was LaMarca, and this girl's father was LaMarca. Her parents both died, and she lives alone in their big house and is lonely. So we take her with us. I smoke, so my cousin and I will go in my car. You three follow in your car."

And we were off that quickly. I followed Nancy over twenty kilometers of treacherous, narrow, winding mountain roads as we climbed the Gran Sasso. On one side was the mountain wall; on the other was a precipitous drop. Only a log rail two feet off the ground kept us from catastrophe. Tilde tried to point out sights of interest along the way. I understood some, but missed most of it.

Joyce kept asking, "What did she say?" And with a death grip on the wheel, I'd answer, "I'm not sure. I think that's an old hermitage of a famous monk." Or, "I think there's something important about that village hanging over the hill, but I don't know what." Then I would look at Tilde, smile and nod, and say, "*Ah, si, si,*" as perspiration soaked my shirt.

We finally reached the lake at Scano around six thirty, as the sun was begin- ning to set. This was a deep mountain lake set at a high elevation. Old-looking resort inns dotted the pine-filled shore, as on a mountain lake in Austria. Even the architecture seemed German. We parked and walked up to a little chapel built into a rock clinging to the steep shore, then walked back to the car and drove up to the village that sits above the lake.

After parking the cars, we walked to a bar, where Tilde bought everyone a cup of espresso (a tarlike, powerfully strong substance served, mercifully, in a thim- ble-sized cup) and what she called a traditional cookie. It was a large round cookie that seemed like a sugar cookie, or shortbread with almonds. Everyone downed the espresso in a minute, and we continued walking around town—aim- lessly, it seemed to me, but I think we were doing the evening *passeggiata*, or maybe just *dolce far niente*.

I was impressed with the narrow streets. With no sidewalks, everyone walked casually in the middle of the street as drivers maneuvered around them. All through Italy, Joyce and I had been jumping out of the way every time we heard approaching cars, but the other walkers seemed oblivious. I pointed this out to Joyce, but she preferred our method for survival.

Finally, we entered a restaurant where the owner seemed to know Nancy. She told us they had excellent lamb. After seating us in a back room, the owner gave the menu verbally—and too quickly for me to understand.

Nancy interpreted: "Would you like some gnocchi? A little lamb? Some salad? Wine?" Then she and Tilde conferred and talked to the owner. He brought pitchers of wine and bottles of water.

Then it started. Trays of food were delivered to our table, serving every dish family style. First came antipasti of prosciutto, another meat I couldn't name, cheeses, fresh-baked regional bread, and a tray of melt-in-your-mouth sausages and artichokes. Next, they brought bowls of gnocchi in spinach and olive oil. I thought we were at the end of the meal, but no. The owner brought a tray the size of Rhode Island piled with grilled lamb and another of pork chops. Then came another type of sausage, then fried potatoes, then salad. I was so stuffed that I thought I was going to faint. Why had we eaten that big lunch earlier? Why did I eat that cookie?

Tilde kept asking if everything was okay. Everything was more than okay; it was absolutely delicious, but I was getting sick from overeating. Then again, I didn't want to offend her by not eating. We ate until ten while I prayed to get through it without collapsing on the floor. Then I had to face the harrowing drive to Bugnara.

Once back in town, we talked for a while in the square before saying good night. Nancy said she would show me the way out. I said that wasn't necessary.

She said, "Okay. Just go down here, and stay left."

After we drove off, I made the first left, but it didn't seem right. As we were going bounce, bounce, bounce, I realized we were going down stone steps into someone's courtyard. I told Joyce to hold on and pray as I made my best effort at a four-way turn on a set of stairs and then bounced, bounced, bounced back up.

As we approached the top, Nancy, Tilde, and the cousin (I never did learn her name.) were running toward us, flailing and yelling, "No! No!"

As I drove past them with a sheepish grin on my sweaty face, Nancy yelled through laughter, "I told you stay left, not turn hard left." What was that supposed to mean?

The ride back to Sulmona was thankfully quiet. We both were stuffed and had headaches, and my mind was swimming from the experience of the day. It was difficult to fall asleep.

After a quick breakfast of cappuccino and pastry at a stand-up bar, we left Sulmona for Bugnara and day two of our visit. This day, we were going to visit my other cousin, Tilde's sister Enza, at her home on the Adriatic Sea. Nancy had said she would not be able to accompany us today, but she would join us for dinner—perhaps an evening out on the town in Sulmona when we returned. Tilde offered more food, which we declined, and after a brief attempt at conversation, we left for Cocullo, the birthplace of my grandfather and, I was to find out, my father. My grandmother and the children had apparently moved to Bugnara to be near her family after my grandfather had gone to America, so that was how my father had come to call Bugnara his hometown.

As we were leaving Tilde's house, another of her cousins walked up the street and stopped to talk. Everyone in this town was related. This woman's father had been a playmate of my father. She asked me a question; thanks to my unreliable grasp of Italian, I thought she asked if I spoke Italian.

I modestly answered, "*Un poco*" (a little).

She and Tilde looked at each other, a little perplexed.

I blushed, thinking my reply had been proof I didn't even speak it a little and said, "Well, *meno di poco*" (very little).

Tilde repeated what the cousin had said with a nervous little laugh. I gave in: "OK. *No, niente*" (no, not at all). Tilde tried one more time, very slowly, and finally I got it. She was asking me if I liked Italy. Alarmed, I burst forth with a flurry of disconnected words saying I had misunderstood her, and I was sorry. I loved Italy—very beautiful ... very, very beautiful! To which they had a good laugh. After a few more words between them (which I didn't understand but probably meant "Where did you find this idiot?"), we left.

On our way out of the village, Tilde had me stop at a little farmhouse by the roadside. She ran in and, after a while, came out with a wheel of pecorino cheese, the sheep's milk cheese made in Abruzzo. The wheel had been made at this little farm and would have been the type of cheese my father would have eaten. She had it shrink-wrapped, so we could take it back on the plane. I smiled and thanked her, thinking, *This strong-smelling little gem will never make it through customs.* But it did.

Cocullo is a pretty little village. Small and remote, about five kilometers from Bugnara, it climbs the side of a steep hill. The entire town is of mud-colored stone—its buildings, roads, and walkways. No wonder my father said Americans lived in shacks; everything in this country was made of stone. He could never get used to the wooden houses in America.

I drove to the center of town into its main square, a small, plain area housing a little church. Tilde approached three people talking by the chapel. She explained we were from America and had come to see my father's birthplace, and that my great grandparents were Gentile and Gizzi. "*Ah, si, si, Gentile e Gizzi,*" they said as they looked at Joyce and me and smiled. These people were well dressed and spoke with a quiet reserve, not the dramatic expressiveness so stereotypically mimicked when people think of Italians.

One of the ladies left shortly to return with a key to the church. This was the church of Madonna della Grazie, built in the Romanesque style in the twelfth century. It was said to have been built on top of a temple dedicated to Jupiter.

Cocullo is known for its feast of San Domenico Abate, celebrated on the first Thursday in May. According to legend, the Sagittario Valley, Cocullo's location, was once menaced by snakes. In the eleventh century, St. Domenic, who was a hermit abbot, came to Cocullo, tamed the snakes, and drove them out of town, similar to St. Patrick's alleged feat in Ireland. Supposedly, the festival was based on St. Domenic's accomplishment.

There is evidence, however, that this ritual actually had pagan origins. It is believed that back in 700 BC, the shepherds prayed to Apollo for help, and he told them to gather up the snakes and drape them over a statue of him, and they would go away. It seems the melding of these two fables has evolved into the practice every year, on feast day, of covering the wooden statue of St. Domenic with live snakes and parading through the streets. On this day, hundreds of tourists fill the town. The rest of the year, it's a sleepy, virtually unvisited village of five hundred inhabitants.

After we passed through the church, Tilde walked with us to a little street behind it and stopped at the house of our great grandfather, Paolo Gentile—the place my grandfather was born. The door was open, and she called out, "Gabriella?" A blond woman of about fifty came out of the house, perspiring and wearing rubber gloves. She obviously had been cleaning. Tilde told her who we were and told us Gabriella's grandfather and my grandfather were brothers. I had not even known he had a brother.

"So she's my cousin too," I said.

"No," said Tilde. "She is the granddaughter of our grandfather's brother." Apparently, the Italians didn't bother with second and third cousins once or twice removed, as we did. I was gaining more insight. Then again, she may have misunderstood my question, or I her answer. I'll never know.

Tilde told Gabriella she wanted to show us the Cathedral of San Domenico Abate, which was built over the cave at the bottom of the village, where St. Domenic had lived. Gabriella said she would go along; she took off her gloves and joined us, leaving the door to the house wide open. We walked to the other end of town to the house of a woman who was to have the key to the cathedral. She wasn't home. Another conversation ensued, and we waited while someone went to the woman's daughter's house to find her. I was impressed with the good nature of these people. I had discovered that throughout this whole Abruzzese region, people would stop what they were doing to help with or to join in on an unplanned activity, even if it meant scrapping an entire day's plans.

While we waited, I noticed stone arches with faded paintings or engravings of a serpent or loops of some sort over the doorways. These had to be throwbacks to the pagan practices, connected to eliminating the snakes. This was indeed an old and storied place. I would have loved to talk more about it with someone, if only there weren't the language barrier. Finally, the old woman came up the hill, went into her house, and came out with a six-inch-long iron key. She walked up the steps of the cathedral, opened the door, and went in, then turned on lights, lit candles, and waited for us for as long as we liked.

When we were back outside, Gabriella and Tilde talked for a while as we walked up another street. Gabriella opened a door into an apartment. I wondered what we were doing. We were due at Enza's at noon, which was an hour and a half drive away. It was now eleven, but Gabriella started making coffee, and Tilde seemed perfectly relaxed. I gathered from Tilde that this was Gabriella's family home. She lived and worked in Rome and used it as a weekend place. This seemed to be the practice with a good many people here. These towns had no work and were full of old people. Younger folks left to work in other places, but kept the family homes and returned on weekends, holidays, and during summer vacation; they probably would retire here someday.

I never was able to figure out who was in my great grandfather's house or why Gabrielle was cleaning it. But we had coffee and cakes and some relaxed conversation. I felt antsy, but Tilde was perfectly at ease. No one seemed to be in a hurry or to get upset over agenda changes. No wonder the Italians' rate of heart attacks and nervous disorders were much lower than ours.

Finally, after good-byes and kisses, we left and merged onto the Autostrada toward Enza's house in the seaside resort town of Roseto degli Abruzzi. For the next hour and a half, our conversation consisted of pointing to a hilltop village and saying, "*Bella.*" The respondent would follow with, "*Si, molta bella.*" Then, after a long pause, someone would point to the mountains and say, "*Grande.*" And so it went until we reached Roseto degli Abruzzi.

Enza and her husband, Flavio, lived in a modern apartment three blocks from the beach. It was at ground level and was reached by walking through an attractive walled garden dominated by a stone barbecue pit and patio.

Enza bore a great resemblance to our daughter Heather. She was in her fifties, attractive, a little taller than Tilde, and blond. She wore black slacks and a v-neck sweater, with a light gray blazer draped over her shoulders. She was pleasant and seemed genuinely happy to see us. She hugged us tightly and kissed us on both cheeks. Then she looked closely at me, turned to Tilde, and said something about, "*Nono Luigi*" while circling my face with her hand. I gathered she thought I looked like my grandfather, which I never thought I did.

Immediately, Enza had us sit at the dining-room table. She brought out wine and glasses and a tray of hors d'oeuvres, insisting we eat. She made a phone call, and within minutes, a dark-haired man with a mustache and glasses bicycled onto their patio. It was Flavio. He was a civil engineer who worked just blocks from their home. Also pleasant and seemingly laid-back, he shook my hand, circled my face with his finger, and said something about "*Nono Luigi*." I was beginning to believe it. The five of us sat there, trying to communicate for a while, until their daughter, Velia, arrived. She was a university student and the only family member who spoke English.

As soon as she walked in, the place came alive. We started on an elementary level. Velia explained that they thought I looked like my grandfather. Also, I have a mole on my cheek. She said her grandmother—my aunt—had the same mole in exactly the same place. They were examining me and asking questions about our family. I have a cousin who is a photojournalist. On a trip to Italy, he had stopped to visit them. They asked about the "*journaliste*." How was he, where was he, what was he doing? They recounted his visit in a way that indicated it had been a momentous event.

Tilde and Enza talked of their mother and how much she missed her brothers. She could never understand why her father had gone with the boys to America and left the girls alone in Italy. They told us we were lucky to have our uncle and cousins in America, because they had no one on the Gentile side of the family in Italy. One time, my father had called and talked to their mother. She cried through the whole conversation, because my father's voice had sounded just like it had as a boy. No wonder my father rarely called. I am certain he felt as badly, but could not—or would not—express it, and therefore chose to avoid the sadness.

They told us our aunt Louise, Tilde and Enza's mother, was a kind and gentle person; our aunt Loretta was stern and somber; our uncle Bill was quiet and gentle; and my dad was "diabolico" (devilish). Then the stories about my dad started. They told one after the other, always with great affection and laughter. I could sense these stories had been told over and over through the years until they became legend. That must have been how my aunt coped with the loss.

Our grandmother had died when my father was twelve. My grandfather had been in America, and Louise, being just fifteen, was given the responsibility of mothering her siblings. Everyone listened to her—except my father. When she would tell him he had to go to school, he would refuse and run up into the mountain with a friend. He spent a great deal of time with his grandfather—his mother's father, Antonio, a tall redhead with one earring and a violent temper. Everyone was afraid of him, except my father. He would play tricks on Antonio and run into the hills to hide until Antonio's anger subsided. For example, Antonio would make their pungent pecorino cheese. He would encase it in a waxy skin in which it had to age for a year. He kept these on a shelf where they were not to be touched until he felt they were ready to be eaten. My father would sneak into the room where they were stored, slice the wax open, scoop the cheese out of the middle, eat it, and replace the wax. After a year of waiting, the big day would come when Antonio was going to cut open the cheese. Taking it from the shelf, he would notice that it was too light; cutting it open would reveal an empty shell. The sight sent him chasing after my father.

As they recounted these stories of my father's devilish nature, it reminded me of the story my father had told about the time he was leaving Italy for America. The mother of one of his friends had approached him on the street and told him she hoped the ship taking him across the Atlantic would sink with him on it. I guess not everyone found his spirited antics cute.

I also learned that, as he was leaving for America, my then-fifteen-year-old father instructed a friend to keep a close eye on his sisters. What this meant was, if they did anything considered to be out of line, the friend was to let my father know. This was typical of the men who left their wives behind. They wanted to make certain the women did not have affairs or act in unacceptable ways. As a result, these women wore black, like widows, and were afraid to take part in the *passeggiata* for fear of having their behavior reported back to their husbands in America. These women were known as white widows and lived this way for the rest of their lives.

As I contemplated this, Enza looked at me and suddenly began to cry. Velia explained that when my grandfather retired and returned to Italy, Tilde was away at college; Enza was at home and spent a great deal of time with him. He told her stories about our family. He and my uncle had lived with us, and upon his return to Italy, he often commented on the goodness of my mother and how hard she worked taking care of them. He also told stories of my brother and me helping him in the garden and other stories of our life in America. As a result, Enza had a strong affection for my grandfather and felt as though she really knew us. That was why our visit had such an emotional effect: she was finally meeting someone she had heard so much about and who had meant a great deal to her grandfather.

Enza was a teacher of literature. Apologizing profusely because she had worked that day and was unable to cook for us, she said they were going to take us to a local restaurant and treat us to a typical meal of their region. This was a definite change in the culture. The old Italians I knew would insist on cooking for you and would be insulted by the action of being taken out to dinner. Possibly now that more Italian women were working outside the house, the act of eating out was becoming more common. But cultures change slowly, and my cousin felt terrible about not making us a meal.

We went to a delightful little waterfront place on the Adriatic that had outside seating under a thatched roof. It was obvious my family was well-known and expected, because we were warmly greeted and led to a very nice table during midafternoon, when the restaurant should have been closed. After a gracious introduction to the proprietor, a sumptuous feast began.

Bottles of white and red wine and water were placed on the table. Trays of seafood were carried out in a seemingly endless line. Every single tray was seafood—no vegetables, no potatoes. Just every type of seafood imaginable—and even some I could never have imagined. We started with antipasti of broiled and steamed clams; then shrimp; sea urchins; squid; mussels; prawns; and anchovies. These were followed by trays of fish with huge, opened mouths called frog fish. By the way, every fish was served in its entirety, complete with full head and dead eyes. Joyce and I found that unpleasant back home, but here, we ate every single thing that was served. Each was more delicious than the one before. Next were trays of scampi almost as big as a lobster. Flavio showed us how to break, clean, and eat these delicacies. I can't imagine what they paid for this feast, but it was the largest I've ever experienced, and indescribably delicious.

Twice during our meal, Flavio's cell phone rang. Each time, he answered it, spoke what seemed to be a few sharp words, and hung up. Looking annoyed, he made a comment and continued to eat. Velia smiled and said, "My father apologizes. He has a few people working for him who cannot make a decision without him."

The conversation moved on to pleasantries. *How sad*, I thought. *It's starting to happen here too.* The cell phone had rudely invaded the sanctity of the Italian home, forcing this man to be at work twenty-four hours a day. But he didn't seem to be carrying it as a badge of importance, instead quickly dismissing the caller. I wondered how long it would be before these kind people would adopt our standard and begin to prioritize the phone call over the people standing before them. I hoped it would never happen.

A few hours later, we left the restaurant and walked along the water to a place selling gelato. We had the best I have ever tasted, then walked a little more. As we walked, Joyce and Velia stayed deep in conversation; the rest of us were quiet. At one point, Flavio said something to Enza that sounded like a reprimand. He said something about how Joyce and Velia were having a great conversation, but no one was talking to me. It's hard to explain, but I was feeling drained—and even a little depressed. Maybe it was nostalgia; maybe it was a feeling of being overwhelmed by the experience. I don't know. I just couldn't think of anything to say, and yet I was flooded with emotions.

We returned to the house for more drinks, questions, and stories. Then Tilde said something that must have expressed her desire to start the ride back. She probably feared the thought of riding again with me in the dark! But before we left, they had gifts for us. I was moved and embarrassed. Joyce and I had talked about giving them gifts but were not sure of the meeting and knew nothing about them. So we decided that if we did get to meet, we would send gifts from America after getting a sense of what they would like.

Tilde gave us a box of the confetti made in Sulmona, then gave Joyce a small box. Inside was a twenty-four-carat gold medallion on a gold chain. Velia explained that in Italy, when a son is married, his mother gives the bride this medallion. Being my family in Italy, Tilde wanted to give it to Joyce. We were both very touched. Enza and Flavio gave us a beautiful china bowl, delicately carved and hand painted by regional potters in a design representative of their province.

We embraced and kissed; Enza cried. We invited them to visit us in America. Enza said that would be wonderful. Velia said it would never happen; her mother was too much of a homebody. But they wanted us to return when we could spend more time. We exchanged home and e-mail addresses. After our tearful good-byes, we started on our return to Bugnara. This time, Tilde slept, but she never released her death grip on the passenger strap above the door.

Back in Bugnara, Nancy and the cousin were waiting in the square. They were ready to go to Sulmona for dinner and a late evening of drinks and chatting. Nancy had asked her brother to burn a CD about Bugnara put out by their visitor's office and gave it to us. I had mentioned earlier that our son Paul thought it would be nice to have a shirt with Bugnara printed on it as a remembrance of his grandfather's hometown. She told me she tried to get us the shirts, but there were none. I knew Nancy had been looking forward to a night out on the town with us. I felt terrible disappointing her, especially after all she had done, but we just could not endure another meal and a late night. We explained we were tired from a long day, and Tilde had to leave early in the morning for Latina. They seemed fine with it. We said our good-byes in the square, complete with hugs and kisses, and then left. An exceptionally warm and touching two days had come to a close.

On the ride back to Sulmona, Joyce and I were quiet, tired, and pensive. I was drained. These people were kind and loving and held our American family in warmth and affection. Why had we never known this? Why had my father never wanted to return? My mother had asked several times if he would like to visit, and he always said, "No. There is nothing for me." I could only think that he felt such deep loss at losing his mother, being away from his sisters, and enduring a life wiped out by death and migration that it would all be too emotional for him. Since he always felt so strongly that a man never cries or shows emotion, he just didn't know how he would handle it—and, therefore, preferred not to face it at all.

I was gaining insight into a side of my father that I had never thought of before. I felt tenderness toward him, along with sorrow for how his life had been split. He had been cheated of a childhood and a family life with two parents and siblings. I wondered whether, if I had known all this growing up, my attitude toward his sternness and gruff manner would have been different. But I would never know.

In the morning, as we were checking out of the Hotel Italia, the owner explained that the velvet gown on a statue in the lobby had been worn by a young woman representing their district of the city in the Chivalrous Tournament. He then gave us a flier from the 2004 event, featuring his picture in full costume, explaining that he had succeeded a long line of ancestors who had participated in the annual event for centuries. Then we were given a beautiful, four-color, glossy booklet of the event containing pages for each district. Turning to the page for Sestrere di Porta Bonomini, he showed us the photo of his daughter wearing the gown. With great pride, he told us these were for us to keep to remember him by, then gave us a warm good-bye. We reluctantly left Sulmona.

But I wasn't yet ready to close the book of my past. There was time to drive the seven kilometers to Pacentro, the childhood home of my grandfather Ciccone—my mother's father. Although there would be no family members to greet us, and we did not have much time to spend, I still wanted to see the village. My grandfather had talked so often of it that I had a visual picture, and I really wanted to walk through those streets, as I had walked through the streets of my father and his father.

We saw on our approach that Pacentro was a picture-perfect postcard of a hill town. At the top of the village, inhabited as early as 800 BC, were the three towers of the fourteenth-century Castello Contelmo. Clustered around its base, stone houses cascaded down the mountainside. Midway down was the square tower of the sixteenth-century Santa Maria Maggiore Church; then more houses continued their cascade down the side of Mount Maiella. This vision could be seen from the main square in Sulmona, and yet it was a world away. Most of the streets were too narrow for cars, and many were made of steps, with some tunneling under others. We parked behind the main square, Piazza del Popolo, and walked. The piazza, dominated by the church and a grand old fountain, was empty. We walked up several flights of steps to the *castello*. It now had a stage built into it and seemed to be used for some sort of performance.

We returned to the square and went into the alimentary. I asked if they had any shirts with "Abruzzo" or "Pacentro" stitched on them. I thought if I couldn't get one from Bugnara, Paul might like one from the birthplace of his great grandfather. The proprietor said no, but there was a store that might carry them. She gave me directions, and Joyce and I walked up a narrow alleyway to what appeared to be a general store. The long, narrow room was stacked to the ceiling with everything imaginable. There were men's and women's clothing, shoes, bolts of fabric, magazines, greeting cards, toys, and notions. A pleasant man who spoke no English showed us polo shirts that had "Pacentro" stitched onto the breast pocket. Perfect! We bought them. As the proprietor was writing up the sale, we found his last name was Rubino, and he had relatives in Monaca, Pennsylvania. My uncle, married to my mother's sister, was a Rubino, and all our Rubino cousins lived in Monaca.

Intrigued, we talked more. His relative's first name did not sound familiar, but he gave us her e-mail address, and we promised to look her up on our return. He gave us a four-color, glossy booklet of their pageant, full of photos of people in elaborate medieval dress. These pictures depicted beautifully costumed and lighted performances at the *castello*. There was an advertisement for his store he thought our Rubino relatives in America would enjoy seeing. I was totally impressed with the pageantry of these little villages. What I had seen of the festivals of Sulmona, Cocullo, and Pacentro seemed every bit as glorious and rich as the Palio of Siena, yet they have gone largely unnoticed by the outside world, because these towns don't receive the tourism and notoriety. I think the festivals of Sulmona, Cocullo, and Pacentro—and I'm sure those of many more little Italian villages—are much better off not receiving the media hype Siena suffers. And I hope it never changes.

I asked permission to take his picture for the relatives back home. With a wide smile, he said certainly—but would I wait until he got his wife from upstairs, so that she could also be in the picture? Now, I must tell you, when we were looking at the shirts, a woman came into the store to buy something, and Mr. Rubino was the only person working. He said hello to her, but spent all his time talking to us and giving us e-mail addresses. Now he had run out of the store to get his wife. When they returned, he asked the woman waiting to be served if she would take the photo of the four of us. She smiled, said certainly, and took the picture. We thanked her and said our good-byes; only as we were leaving did he ask her what she wanted. Once again, I was astounded by the laid-back sense of leisure with which everyone I met in the province of Abruzzo went through the day. In America, that woman would have been outraged at his seeming inattentiveness and probably would have left, vowing never to return. This woman was now having an amiable conversation with Mr. Rubino. What made them so pleasant? Was it something in the water?

After a delightful, unhurried, and inexpensive lunch, we left Pacentro for our ride to Sorrento. As we drove down into the Sulmona valley and back out to the south, Joyce and I talked of our few days in this lovely place. We looked at each other and at the same time said, "I could live here."

I had said that more than once on this trip; you might be thinking, *This guy could live anywhere.* Well, I couldn't live just anywhere; I don't think I could live in Patterson, New Jersey. But I really loved this valley, the city of Sulmona, and the villages of my family. It may have been partly because I had connected with my family and felt a deep sense of heritage and nostalgia. But also, it was the place and its people. In addition to being visually beautiful, the village was warm and welcoming and unquestioning, like no other place. It was out of the mainstream tourist haunts, yet had sophistication and vibrancy mixed with calm simplicity. Joyce felt it, and I felt it. We were more relaxed than we had been in a long time. We hated to leave this peaceful haven.

Eye-Popping Beauty and Decadence along the Amalfi Coast

I had wanted to see Caserta and its castle, which was supposed to rival Versailles, but after spending time in Pacentro, we decided to bypass Caserta and drive directly to Sorrento. We had another absolutely beautiful drive out of the Abruzzeze and Molizeze mountains and got back onto the Autostrada, running through a flat plane headed for Naples. We merged onto the wrong leg of the Autostrada outside of Naples, which added another half hour to our trip, but it wasn't that bad; the detour just didn't seem to affect our mood. We also decided not to stop in Naples. I had heard too many bad things about it. My aunt told us to stay out of Naples. Well, what she said was, "The Napolitano will steal your socks without taking off your shoes." The guidebooks said something about Naples being an emotional and complex place that may take a little getting used to. I paraphrase, but you get the idea. I didn't have the time or desire to wait for Naples to grow on me and maybe get robbed in the process, so we opted to bypass it and head straight to Sorrento, which the guidebooks said was loaded with charm. Perhaps we'd save Naples for another time.

The drive through the outskirts of the city on the Autostrada was tense enough. In addition to horrendous traffic and maniacal drivers, we got to enjoy miles of cold, concrete, bunker-style apartment buildings loaded with graffiti. What a dramatic contrast to the pristine beauty we had enjoyed only a few hours before. Once again, I was struck by the ugliness of contemporary Italian urban housing and the way it contradicted the natural beauty of the countryside and the appeal of older architecture. I knew I couldn't—or wouldn't—live here. Even powerful Vesuvius looming on the distant left wasn't enough of a distraction to make me want to spend much time there—or even slow the car.

Barely past Naples, we exited the Autostrada into mind-numbing, nerve-racking traffic. As we crawled through tourist-packed seaside neighborhoods, I kept thinking we were entering Sorrento, only to come upon a sign stating we were exiting a place with an unrecognizable name. Narrow, dirty streets were jammed with massive tour buses, cars, Vespas, bicycles, and pedestrians. I didn't know whether these people were darting in front of our car out of frustration or if the traffic was making them suicidal. I lusted for a hotel with an appearance of reasonable safety and a parking space.

Finally, on the fringe of downtown Sorrento, we came upon a hotel with three stars over the door and a sign that advertised free parking. I quickly swerved into an unloading area about the size of my computer keyboard, cracked the door enough to squeeze out without being dragged down the street by a passing tour bus, and went into a reasonably nice lobby. The Hotel Girasole had a vacancy. I asked to see the room; this time, I wasn't taking any chances. It was a delightful little room with shiny terrazzo floors, a little balcony overlooking the pool, and a garden of lemon trees where we could have our breakfast—which was included, along with a covered parking space. We could enjoy all this for one hundred euros—twenty less than the Hotel Anna! I ran back down to the lobby and quickly told them I would take it before they changed their minds or told me it was a mistake.

Even though we were nearly a mile from the center of Sorrento, we walked into town, happy to be out of the car. It was evening now, and Sorrento was busy and noisy—not the idyllic seaside resort I had imagined. We walked the main street, Corso Italia, a traffic-choked commercial stretch housing every clothier, jeweler, and shoe shop known to mankind. It was not restful, so we decided to try the pedestrian-only alleyways around it. Via S Cesaria was the main one, with several others crossing it. They were all loaded with souvenir shops, leather shops, and places selling their famous inlaid wooden objects and pottery, not to mention scores of stores selling limoncello.

Because it was totally covered with lemon trees, the Sorrentine Peninsula was considered the lemoncello capital of the world. Limoncello is a delectable liquor made from lemon peels, sugar, and alcohol. The people of that region like to chill it almost to the point of freezing, then drink it as an aperitif and a digestive. It was for sale everywhere and at all prices.

In a little, out-of-the-way alley, we came upon an appealing restaurant with garden seating under a cluster of lemon trees. We stopped there and enjoyed some wine and a light dinner to soft strains of Italian music. This meal provided just the relaxation fix we needed. After dinner, we walked around town, looking for the water. I expected Sorrento to be a beach town, but it seemed this town, built on a bluff, wasn't really oriented to the water. People had to either take taxis or walk down steep roads that were now totally dark to get to the water—and even then, they would find no beaches. The waterfront was a mass of docks from which boats departed for Capri and countless other ports along the coast. We decided to head back to our room and have a glass of wine on our balcony. It was a pleasant way to end the evening; from there, we could see the water in the distance.

It was cool in the morning, so we decided to have breakfast in the hotel dining room, which featured an entire wall of sliding glass that opened onto the lemon orchard. Breakfast was very nice and had us feeling refreshed. The surroundings were pleasant, but we were anxious to get started for Positano.

We exited Sorrento on Via del Campo, past posh resorts built out over rocky cliffs. These had the views of the Bay of Naples we were looking for in town, but they were a good hike up a busy commercial road, which did not seem attractive to us—nor did their prices. We followed a narrow country road all the way out to the tip of the Sorrentine Peninsula, then back along the other side, eventually joining the famous (or infamous) Amalfi Drive. We had heard many stories about this drive and the maniacal Italian drivers who would intimidate the most hardened adventurer. To my surprise, the drive was not frightening, but phenomenally gorgeous.

We were in heaven, soaring above the sea with the eagles. To our right, the deep, royal blue waters of the Tyrannian Sea below glistened and gently caressed sailing vessels and yachts. We feasted on this view. To our left, the majestic, white, rocky limestone cliffs rose into the sky, dotted with stone farmhouses and an occasional glimpse of the road ahead, which wound in and out of view. Straight ahead and all around, birds were flying at eye height—not above us, but with us. As we drove, we found ourselves in the air, then thrust back through a tunnel and out into the air again, curving around stone cliffs. We had to go slowly and sometimes stop for a passing tour bus, but it wasn't frightening—it was exhilarating. On the sea side was a stone wall built at about knee height to keep the driver from going over the edge. This was by far less gut-wrenching than our drive through Independence Pass in Colorado.

The Independence Pass road was narrow and carved into the edge of the mountain, doing a series of switchbacks to get us to the summit and the Continental Divide. It had no guardrails, and the cliff dropped at the white line defining the edge of the road—not an inch to spare. I concentrated on nothing but getting to the top. I had visions of us plummeting to our demise. I remember my hands were clammy and my knuckles white as I clenched the steering wheel, staring intently at the inside of the road in fear that a glance at the cliff edge would pull us over. The Amalfi Drive was a cakewalk by comparison.

Occasionally, we could see restaurants nestled in little coves, with stone stairs either leading down to them from a road above, or up from the water. Clusters of little fishing villages clung to these steep cliffs, with gardens and lemon trees terraced above. Rather than tense, it was a relaxing experience, although I must admit I was driving slow enough that Joyce could enjoy the view without worrying that I would hurl us to our demise.

We arrived in Positano and immediately found the garage that our hotel had sent printed directions to. Positano has been described as a vertical town. Its houses and buildings are square, flat-roofed, and walled mostly in white stucco, with many arches that give them a Moorish look. They start at the water's edge and seem to be built on top of one another, stacking up the sides of steep, gray and white stone cliffs. It was a very dramatic and romantic town. There were no museums, art treasures, ruins, or archeological sites—just sun and sea and visual beauty. The shops and restaurants promoted the pure decadence of seaside fun and relaxation.

Taking our bags from the car, we walked out onto Via Pasitea—the one-way, one-car wide main road that ran down through town and back up the opposite end. It was only a hundred-yard walk down the road to the Albergo Punta Regina—which, like all the buildings of town, was built right to the edge of the road. There were no sidewalks on long stretches of this road; existing sidewalks were too narrow even for one person, making them almost unusable. People just walked out on the street as drivers skillfully threaded through them.

We climbed up stairs lined with tiny lights and past a glass door, which slid open as we approached. We accepted the mute invitation and proceeded into a lovely vaulted and arched lobby of Moorish influence with glossy tile floors, massive vases filled with fresh flowers, and a magnificently ornate antique walnut reception desk. The most pleasant, attractive young woman greeted us, and, although we were early, said our room would be ready in a few minutes. If we would like, we could wait on the rooftop terrace. On cue, a handsome, very pleasant young man appeared immediately and introduced himself as Alessandro—apparently a very popular name in Italy. He led us to the terrace, seated us at a table with a heart-stopping view of the sea and the buildings of Positano tumbling down to it, then quickly presented two cool drinks. Within ten minutes, Alessandro reappeared to announce our room was ready and took us to it, where our bags were waiting.

The Punta Regina was a four-star, boutique-style hotel, and it deserved every star. The dazzling white converted four-story palazzo, which had just opened in the 2000 season, was loaded with overflowing flower boxes and had only thirteen rooms. Some rooms were suites that had full terraces and outdoor Jacuzzis. Ours was their standard room, but I would classify it as a junior suite. It had a vaulted ceiling, a writing desk tucked into an arched alcove, a tiled floor, a sitting area with couch, a minibar and safe, a king bed, and a lavish tile and marble bath. This was all set off by French doors leading to a balcony framed with vining flowers and the same gorgeous view of the boat-dotted sea, the medieval tower Clavel, and La Galli Island beyond.

It was a beautiful October day, with temperatures in the mid eighties. We decided to change into shorts and sandals and walk down to Spiaggia Grande, the main beach and hub of town. Tamara, the delightful woman at the desk, told us how we could take steps down to the beach, but would probably like to walk the road back up to the hotel. We did that, and through our entire stay, we chose never to take the steps up. There were 380 of them from our hotel to the beginning of the little pedestrian shopping lanes around Spiaggia Grande.

We decided to eat lunch at the popular Buca di Bacco (Cellar of Bacchus—Bacchus was the Greek and Roman God of wine), which was a highly acclaimed restaurant in a hotel of the same name. At the turn of the last century, it had been the haunt of artists and intellectuals, and now, even though it was overrun by tourists and a bit pricey, it was still written about in the tour books for its fresh seafood delivered directly from the boats each day. We sat out on the vine-covered terrace overlooking the busy walk, beach, and sea beyond, enjoying great food and fantastic views.

To digest, we started walking back up to the hotel, this time starting through the pedestrian-only Via dei Mulini, which was lined with tony dress and shoe shops, ceramic and art shops, and shops selling everything you could possibly make out of lemon. Via dei Mulini spilled out onto Via Cristoforo Columbo, which became Viale Pasitea—the narrow, twisting main street of Positano that dropped down, then climbed up from one end of town to the other and back onto the Amalfi Drive. These too were lined with shops and restaurants and hotels enough to occupy us for the entire week if I wasn't careful.

Joyce decided to buy a very chic Positano style (whatever that means) wrap for herself at one of the tony shops, where the clerks reluctantly approach while looking as if they smell something really bad. Of course, the woman warmed to us as the prospect of a sale became more of a reality. Then the unthinkable happened: Joyce's Visa card was rejected. "That can't be!" she exclaimed. "We always pay our Visa off each month; there are not that many charges on it."

The woman called Visa for Joyce and handed her the phone. She found Visa had put a hold on the account because charges were appearing rapidly along a path through Italy. That activity threw up a flag, because the card could have been stolen by thieves who were using it as they moved about. Joyce assured them we were the people moving about, as we were in Italy for a month. Visa apologized, then advised us to notify them when we were going to be doing extensive traveling, so they would not be suspicious when a series of charges appeared to be moving about. Then they reactivated her card. Very pleased that Visa was protecting us so vigilantly, Joyce concluded the purchase, and we were on our way.

The heat was getting to me; everywhere I looked, there were bottles of every size and shape of limoncello. Feeling quite sophisticated, I passed all the tony and expensive limoncello shops and stopped to buy a bottle at a fraction of the cost in a little alimentary. Back at the room, we put it in the freezer of our minibar.

When it was chilled, we sat out on our balcony, sipping glasses of it, reading and thoroughly enjoying what had become our favorite pastime: *dolce fare niente*. When we got tired of that, we took a nap, then went back out on the balcony for another glass. We witnessed the most beautiful sunset of our lives before heading out for our evening meal and another walk.

The tour books had mentioned a ferry service between Positano and Capri. On our way out, we stopped at the desk, asked Tamara if she had a schedule, and told her we would like to go there one day during the week. In her most pleasant and flowery manner, she explained the ferry schedule was limited during the off-season—which this was. However, tour boats ran all the time from Positano, and for the little extra expense, they stopped at places like the Blue Grotto, which was a must-see for everyone visiting Capri. It would be much more convenient for us, she explained before offering to take care of the booking. Then she cautioned us that these boats would not make the trip in rainy weather, and other than tomorrow, the rest of the week called for rain. We told her to book us for tomorrow.

For forty euros each, we had reservations on the Blue Star, scheduled to leave at 9:30 AM from the dock at Spiaggia Grande. Under an overcast sky, the Blue Star, a thirty-foot boat with no cabin, pulled up to the dock. It was driven by a short, deeply tanned man in shorts—no shirt or shoes—and a very limited command of English. He steered the boat with his feet so that his hands could be free to help him narrate our trip. Twelve of us boarded the boat: two couples from Chicago, two teenaged brothers from Salt Lake City who said their parents insisted they make the trip, a couple from Ireland, and a young Italian couple that spoke no English ... although that was only a guess, since they barely emerged from severe lip locks except to get off and on the boat.

Despite the gray sky, the trip was pleasant. The Amalfi cliffs seemed even higher from the water. We were dwarfed by these majestic rock cliffs shooting straight up into the air and disappearing into the low clouds. From the water, the Amalfi Drive looked like a ribbon that had been dropped along the cliff's edge, and the tour buses and cars looked like toys. As Capri came into sight, it looked mysterious and imposing, its limestone mass swelling out of the water and into the mist.

We stopped first at the Green Grotto, where the captain told us to look for images in the rock face (none of which I could find) and told some barely comprehensible stories—folklore, I guess. Then he took us through the hole in the Faraglioni, the three rocks off the island coast that Homer was believed to have referred to as the sirens who lured sailors to their deaths upon the rocks.

We continued around the island to the greatest rip-off of all time, the Blue Grotto. Every tour book and every person who has ever gone to Capri insists the Blue Grotto is the must-see of your trip. Let me tell you how it worked. It was only possible to get to the grotto by boat—for which, of course, there was a fee. Our fee to get to the grotto was included in the price of our day excursion, but it was also possible to get boats from either of the two marinas of Capri, or from Sorrento, Naples, and anywhere else along the coast.

As we approached the grotto, we could see a number of boats approaching, hovering, and leaving the mouth of the grotto, which was a cave with a three-foot opening. Circling these boats and going in and out of the cave were about a dozen small rowboats that had a driver and could take four passengers. As we pulled up to the cave entrance, we were besieged by these little rowboats and their drivers, who yelled at the top of their lungs, "Come! See the Blue Grotto, hurry, hurry! Men! Sit on the floor! Ladies! Sit between the legs! Hurry! Hurry!" as they pulled us from our boat onto theirs. Once we were thrown into our little boat, the driver quickly paddled over to another boat—a kind of floating ticket booth—where men collected the ten-euro-per-person fee. As they were getting their money from us, our driver was instructing us that we would be expected to give him a generous tip at the end or the tour for his work, that the fee we were now paying was not the end of our obligation, and we should understand that before we went any farther.

Quicker than a speeding bullet, we were at the entrance, and as the waves jostled us up and down, he shouted for us to lower our heads, lest they be cut off from not clearing the entrance while he pulled on a chain that, in a quick whoosh, shot us through the opening and into the cave. Inside, it was dark except for the water, which appeared to be dyed blue and backlit. We got in line with the others who were in that thirty-foot cave and made one circle, like the little duckies in a children's ride at the amusement park. Before you could say "rip-off," he was pulling on that chain and shooting us back into the open sea and back to our boats. He collected his tip—wham, bam, thank you ma'am.

We must have had a kind rowboat driver, because after the two couples from Chicago were thrown back onto our boat, they relayed the story of their driver. He not only told them they must pay him a tip, but it had to be ten euros per person. Then they asked him to take their picture, for which he charged ten euros. The one man took the driver's picture, and ... have you guessed it? He charged them another ten euros for taking his picture. So these trusting folks from the Midwest paid one hundred euros, or about $124 American, for a five-minute screw job, complete with photos.

As we were telling our stories, someone wondered why everyone tells you it is a must to see the Blue Grotto. The only thing we could think was they didn't want to be the only ones who were dumb enough to have gotten ripped off. But honestly, with all the trouble going on in the world before our trip and the tension we had been feeling and the killing the dollar was taking, I had decided early on not to stress over money. Not very far into our trip, I had stopped using my converter. I figured we would just enjoy this trip and calculate the conversions once at home. And we really were enjoying each experience—even the absurdity of the Blue Grotto.

Our boat continued around the island to Marina Grande, the main landing area for all ferries, shuttles, and boats. The place was jammed with boats and hydrofoils arriving and leaving. Capri Village was at the top of a bluff overlooking the marina. At water level, the docks were surrounded by overpriced restaurants and shops selling every tacky souvenir imaginable. The place was loaded with tour groups milling around. Shop and restaurant owners stood in front of their establishments, hawking their wares and trying to pull in passers-by. The drivers of taxis everywhere did the same thing.

The boys from Salt Lake City told us their parents had been there earlier in the week; the couple had taken one of the taxis up the hill to Capri village and paid seventy-five euros for the half-mile ride. I told them I read in my trusty Frommer's book that it was possible to get a round-trip ticket for the funicular for just four euros. We went to the ticket booth, joined a line that snaked out into the street, got our tickets, and then waited about half an hour in line for the three-minute ride … kind of like a Disney experience.

Once at the top, we fought the crowds to squeeze into Capri's main square, Piazza Umberto I, which the guidebooks described as a grand living room lined with cafés. I had never been in a living room like this. Every seat at every table at every café was filled, and what seemed like thousands of people were jammed into the square—sitting on the steps of the cathedral, walking around the piazza and through the tables, knocking people at the tables on their heads with cameras and bags. I looked at this scene and had visions of the snake pit. This was October. What was it like in the summer?

The narrow, pedestrian-only alleys shooting out in every direction from the Piazza were just as packed with day trippers moving in and out of designer shops and stores of every imaginable kind—except the reasonably priced kind. Architecturally, the town was beautiful, and the views from this clifftop village were fantastic, but they were buried behind the crush of people filling every space. This was supposed to be the haunt of celebrities. I could only think they must have been hiding in their rooms in the swank hotels, or in some out-of-the-way villas, until the day trippers left at sunset. Maybe then they could come out without being accosted by hordes of autograph-hungry tourists.

We went into a visitor's center, and I bought a walking map of the island. Several self-guided walking tours looked good. We had only four hours until our boat departed for Positano, so we chose a walking tour that looked as if it could be completed in enough time that we wouldn't feel rushed. We would walk to Mount Tiberius and the Villa Jovis.

I checked my watch to make sure we would have enough time. It had stopped running. When had that happened? I realized I couldn't remember when I had last looked at it. Should I look for a jeweler and have it repaired? Forget it. If I hadn't noticed when it stopped, I didn't need it. I spent the rest of our stay in Italy without a watch; I enjoyed not needing to know the time every minute.

The walk was uphill all the way, but delightful. As we left the clamor of the shops behind, the narrow alleys became less crowded and then empty as they wound and turned past old, beautiful, yellow and ocher colored villas resting behind stone walls. These walls dripped with the bright colors and sweet smells of bougainvillea, jasmine, and oleander. The last leg of the walk left all signs of civilization behind, and we trod along a footpath with dramatic 360-degree views of the island and surrounding sea.

Suddenly, out of the calm, we could hear the growing noise of a helicopter building to a defining clatter as it surfaced directly over our heads, carrying a load of steel beams. It descended to drop its payload onto the ground fifty feet from us. We peered over a chain-link fence to see three workmen who would direct the chopper to a spot, disconnect the beams from the chain hanging from under the chopper, and signal it off again. We later found out that an exclusive resort hotel was being built on that site. The only way to get the materials to the site was by ship to the foot of the cliffs and then by helicopter. The builders obviously were not too worried about the tourists walking in their pathway. I'm sure Tiberius had included a few first-century tourists in the cement mix of old Vila Jovis; what were a few more? What a shame that this pristine spot was soon to be just another money-making stop to jam more tourists into.

We continued to the highest point on the island, and the ruins. The Villa Jovis was the largest, most sumptuous of Emperor Tiberius's many villas on Capri, and apparently the place of much debauchery—and the flinging of a few people who displeased him over the cliffs to the sea below.

There was a fee to enter. I went into the small gift shop and asked the attendant, in my best Italian, for two tickets. He asked, "U.S.?"

I said yes, and Joyce asked, "How did you know we were from the U.S.?"

Even though he would have detected an accent, how much could he have gotten from my, "*Buon giorno*," and "*Due?*"

He answered, "I've been selling these tickets for years, and I can tell where people are from when they walk in the door."

"How?" I asked.

"Americans are always happy, the British are sad, the Germans look angry, and the French ... they look like they have been drinking too much wine." Another bit of simple Italian observation on life; and the more I thought about it, the truer it was. From then on, Joyce and I would see people walking by with a certain look on their faces and say, "They must be German," or "They must be British." And when they spoke in their native tongue, we were often proved right.

Outside the gift shop, a very enterprising Italian was selling poorly Xeroxed copies of a map of the ruins, which we chose not to buy, since the walk through took about five minutes, and I doubted I would get lost. The ruins were interesting, and the view out to the bays of Naples and Salerno and the entire Amalfi Coast would have been fantastic if it had not been so overcast that we could barely see the boats in the water directly below.

We walked back down the path, past the still-working helicopter, past Cartier, Prada, and Fendi, and onto the funicular. At Marina Grande, we still had an hour before departure time, but absolutely no interest in the tacky gift shops. Knowing it would be a rip-off, we chose a table along the dock and ordered a cool, bad-tasting, and very expensive orange granite with gin, which was recommended by our waiter, while we watched the give and take of tourists and merchants.

Back at Positano by six, we showered and felt too tired to make the trek back down into town for dinner. Instead, we walked to a little trattoria just up the street from the hotel called the Mediterranio, then sat outside and had some wine, a pizza, and salad. It was very pleasant and filled with locals. They all seemed to know each other. The owner got out his guitar and began singing while strolling the tables. Unlike the usual tourist trap of strolling singers, no one collected money, and all the patrons sang along with him. It was a perfect way to end the evening.

On Saturday, we wanted to go to Ravello, which the tour books referred to as a clifftop paradise and one of the loveliest resort towns on the Amalfi coast. We started the day with our usual ritual: breakfast up on the rooftop terrace at our favorite table on an elevated balcony overlooking the sea. Breakfasts here were an event in themselves. The tables were always set with white linen and delicate china with a floral print, and every table was centered with a glass bowl full of fresh-cut floating flowers. Inside a glass-enclosed gazebo was the buffet, loaded with cereals; breads; croissants; a different, freshly made pastry every morning; orange juice, green apple juice; and fresh fruit, including huge, juicy figs.

There was always an English printed newspaper to read. That morning, I chose the *New York Times*. The presidential debates were going on, and I hated missing them, but the news coverage of them was excellent. It seemed the Europeans were far more interested in world news than the Americans. Every person seemed knowledgeable about and conversant with what was happening. When we discussed the world situation with any Italian, we found they were greatly aware and analytical without being emotional or getting into name calling. We found no hostility toward us, and their opinions about the United States and the war were factual and nonjudgmental. I found it very refreshing and wished we could have intelligent conversations at home without the temper displays and juvenile name-calling. I guess the Italians reserved all their emotion for the road.

Speaking of the road, our friend Alessandro, who had showed us to the roof top upon our arrival, advised that we may want to get a bus to Ravello rather than risk driving. Many claimed the road to Ravello was far more frightening than the Amalfi Drive. We heard this from more than one person. After breakfast, we stopped at the desk and asked Tamara for advice. She politely said with her usual smile, "You know how to drive a car? You drove the Amalfi Drive to get here? You can drive to Ravello. Just go slowly." As always, she was right.

The drive was incredible—the most frightening of all Italy, but still not as bad as Independence Pass. The Amalfi Drive is narrow, winding, hilly, and heavily traveled, but slow because of the tour buses and because it passes through every little town. However, after going through the extremely congested town of Amalfi, we had to take a secondary road they called "The Dragon" because of the way it snaked through the hills as it climbed 1,155 feet to Ravello. This road was only one car lane wide, but had two-way traffic. At every bend in the road were those convex mirrors that didn't help at all. When a car approached, one had to stop while the other maneuvered around it. Of course, the motorcycles would weave around cars so closely that if I had my elbow resting on an open window, I could have knocked the driver off and over the edge—which, at times, seemed an attractive idea. The road was so narrow that we had to pull our side mirror into the side of the car to avoid hitting the stone hillside.

The drive was worth every destroyed nerve ending. Ravello was beautiful and serene. Although the place was a little busy, its crowds could not compare with those of the other towns. It was a very genteel town. People were well dressed and quiet. Calm seemed to hang over the town square, complete with the requisite churches, cafés, and terraces overlooking the hills and valleys around. It was as though we were standing in a bird's nest.

We toured the Villa Rufolo, the ruins of a villa built by a patrician family in the eleventh century that had served as residence to several popes. For a four-euro ticket, we were able to walk through the Moorish cloister and tower and the fabulous gardens loaded with flowers, palms, lilies, and bougainvilleas. These gardens had inspired composer Richard Wagner to write the second act of *Parsifal*. When he saw them, it is said he exclaimed, "I have found the magical garden of Klingsor." It is here that the summer music festival of Ravello is held. Concerts are performed on a stage built in the midst of these gardens, backed by the dramatic view of the sea and Bay of Salerno.

A local resident recommended a restaurant called Salvatore for lunch. It was just down the road from Villa Rufolo and perched on the cliff edge with the same dramatic views. We sat out on the terrace and were immediately given a complimentary antipasto of crème di ricotta with pepper and olive oil, which we devoured along with some great crusty bread. We then enjoyed servings of stuffed pork and steak with hazelnut mashed potatoes. Everything was superb.

Next, we walked a narrow, stepped pathway out to the very edge of the cliff to the Villa Cimbrone. This fifteenth-century villa, one of Ravello's most exquisite, at one time was owned by a wealthy Englishman who renovated it to its present glory. While here, he entertained such literary luminaries as Henrik Ibsen, D. H. Lawrence, Virginia Woolf, and Tennessee Williams. It was later made into, and still is, a hotel. This was where Greta Garbo had a tryst in 1938 with Leopold Stokowski. The villa is surrounded by gardens punctuated with statues, ancient ruins, and recreations of Greek and Roman temples. These lush gardens extend to the cliff edge, where one has a sense of being airborne. Local resident Gore Vidal has proclaimed it the most beautiful view in the world. I'd be hard pressed to find one better.

Back in Positano and tired from the drive, we stopped at the town's version of a jazz club. It was very close to the hotel and had tables and couches arranged in a garden, which looked relaxing. We had some wine, a cheese tray, and bowls of soup while enjoying soft strains of jazz. It was far too early for the nightclub crowd, so the venue offered a nice way for us to unwind all alone. Then we went back to our room to finish a peaceful night on our balcony with some heavily chilled limoncello, a sky full of stars, and the waves crashing on rocks below.

Sunday morning, while enjoying another great breakfast, we heard bells chime. We walked about fifty yards down our street to a tiny chapel for mass.

This little Church of Saint Catherine had only eight rows of four chairs on each side of a tiny aisle. It was filled mostly with elderly ladies. There was no organ, and everyone sang a cappella very loudly. It was a bit of Old World charm in the middle of modern-day tourism. We spent a lazy Sunday reading, napping, and drinking limoncello.

In the evening, we went out in time to take part in the *passeggiata* and ate dinner at Palazzo Murat's beautiful bougainvillea-draped patio and garden. The palazzo had been built in the early eighteenth century and used as a summer residence by Joachin Murat, king of Naples and Napoleon's brother-in-law. It has since been converted into a hotel and excellent restaurant.

We entered the restaurant through a stone wall that enclosed the palazzo and garden, along a stone pathway lined with lit torches. Soft Italian music was piped into the garden, and the waiters were very quiet and subtly attentive. The scent of the blooming bougainvillea filled the air. Our waiter told us that due to the unusually hot October, the bougainvillea had already bloomed twice before. As we were finishing our meal, it began to softly rain. The waiters quietly moved about, opening large, freestanding umbrellas that covered the tables and patrons. The service never missed a beat; no one jumped up to run for cover. It was blissful.

By the time we were ready to start our walk back up the hill, the rain had stopped. People began quietly coming out into the street onto damp walkways. We stopped to buy another bottle of limoncello, then walked hand in hand back to our room. It was a very romantic evening.

On Monday morning, we awoke at eight thirty to the cozy sound of rain falling outside our opened, but shuttered, doors. By the time we started up toward the roof for breakfast, the rain had stopped, but because everything on the terrace was wet, we were served under the cover of the gazebo. We read *USA Today* as Alessandro served us seconds on the cappuccinos, then headed down to the room to watch the BBC coverage of the presidential campaign and debates.

By noon, the sun came out, exposing the clearest day since we arrived. I walked out on the balcony and saw that mountains were visible to the tops, along with clear blue sky beyond. We decided to walk into town and go through the cathedral, Santa Maria Assunta, whose multicolored, majolica-tiled dome dominated the town view. From there, we walked along the far right of Spaiggia Grande along a narrow stone walk and steps that were carved into the cliff side. This dramatic passageway was called Via Positanesi d'America in honor of the many Positanesi who immigrated to the United States. This lovely seaside walk took us past the Torre Trasita, the most distinctive of Positano's three medieval defense towers built on the water's edge.

Beyond the tower, we climbed stairs up to Lo Guarracino, an idyllic arbor-covered restaurant dramatically clinging to the cliffside. There, we sat at a table that was cantilevered over the water and ate the best seafood of our entire trip—perhaps tied with, but not as plentiful as, our cousins' meal at Roseto. I had a seafood risotto, and Joyce had seafood pasta. They both had mussels, clams, sea urchins, calamari, shrimp, and squid. Joyce found a stone in hers—proof that it was served straight from the sea to her dish.

Two couples at the next table started talking to us. The one couple had lived in Erie, Pennsylvania, and both now lived outside of Charleston, South Carolina. We exchanged e-mail addresses and regular addresses, talked of wine tastings and cooking festivals, and promised to get in touch when back in the States.

After lunch, we continued our walk along Via Positanesi d'America to Spiaggia del Fornillo, an out-of-the-way beach that was much smaller and less crowded than Spiaggia Grande. This was the one we could see from our hotel balcony. It was a delightful little place. The beach was made of black stones the size of golf balls mixed with smaller stones. The cliff rose directly behind. At the cliff's base were wooden, shack-style restaurants or bars with wooden decks in front—much more rustic than at Spiaggia Grande. From the decks, wooden walks ran to the water. Wood and canvas beach chairs lined each side of these walks, along with tented changing booths.

The restaurants seemed to control the beach area in front of them and collected a fee from anyone wanting to use a beach chair. These places seemed to be patronized by locals. We recognized a few from the trattoria we had visited a few nights ago. They were sitting on the deck, playing cards. We decided to go for a swim at this beach tomorrow.

Having eaten too much at lunch, we decided to go light for dinner. We walked to Spiaggia Grande and had pizza and wine at Chez Black, a famous Positano eatery right in the center of all the action. Along with everyone else, we sat at little tables facing the crowds walking by on the busy beachfront boardwalk. It was another delightful evening of doing nothing.

A thunderstorm rolled in through the night. I got up and opened the shutters for a wondrously cozy night of sleep. We dined on another breakfast under the gazebo as the sun came out. Tamara gave us a canvas bag containing two beach towels, and we walked down three hundred stairs to Spiaggia del Fornillo.

We chose to spend our day at Bagno Pucillino, where the charge was ten euros for two chairs and an umbrella, along with use of the changing room and showers. This was a real bargain—half the charge at Spiaggia Grande. This little cove was really quiet. The few other sunbathers were Italian, German, or British. We spent the whole day there, having drinks at our chairs, only moving enough to get to a table on the deck to eat lunch while watching sailboats bobbing at their moorings. An occasional water scooter splashed by, adding just a touch of action to the idyllic landscape.

Sooner or later, it had to end. This was our last night in paradise; we had to do something special. We had noticed at the far end of Spiaggia Grande a nightclub set in a cave inside a huge rock outcropping that plunged into the water. Upon inquiry we found it was the very hip—and, it seemed, the only—nightclub in Positano, aptly named Music on the Rocks. We were told it was Sharon Stone's favorite hangout when she was in town. I think that was meant to impress, but it didn't. What did impress was the outdoor rooftop (or rather, rocktop) restaurant perched on the top of this gigantic rock. It was supposed to be very expensive and exclusive, but had the most commanding view of all Positano. It was glass enclosed, I guess to protect against the wind, but had no roof.

I figured why not. We would throw caution—and our checkbook—to the wind. "Let's go all out our last night here and have dinner at Le Terrazze," I suggested. Tamara thought our choice was a bit extravagant, and perhaps not worth the price we would have to pay. But this time, we did not heed her advice. She called and made our reservation. We dressed in the best clothes we had taken on this trip and started out on our last *passeggiata* at Positano.

To get to the restaurant, we had to walk to the very end of Spiaggia Grande and follow a torch-lit stone path and steps out around the rock edge that jutted into the water, and then into the cave, which was actually the nightclub. Once inside this neon-lit, couch-lined Flintstone lounge, we were taken up spiral stone stairs that wound around the outside of the rock face to the very top. At the top was a bar with polished stone floors, a white cloth retractable roof, and a glossy white grand piano. We were led down two steps to the circular, glass-walled, open-air, torch-lit dining room and seated at white wrought-iron chairs around a white linen-clothed table with a view of the entire cliffside town before us. Waves crashed on the rocks below, and stars filled the sky above.

The waiters were extremely attentive; there must have been one per table. Every one of them was young, tall, dark, and handsome in an Italian gigolo sort of way. They wore tight, pale blue denim slacks and white embroidered shirts. Customers at the tables looked very much alike: old, balding men with young, extremely well-built and bored-looking blond women of the plastic variety. The scene was complete when the piano player, dressed in white, began playing. We were truly out of our league here. But the view, wine, food, and entertainment were worth whatever this night was going to cost.

Actually, the food and service were exquisite. For starters we were given complimentary champagne, shrimp tempura, and caviar on julienned carrots. We ordered a bottle of white wine from the Campania region and shared an antipasto of mushrooms stuffed with speck ham, drizzled with olive oil and herbs, and then grilled. Then we had fresh white (what else) fish from the area, grilled with herbs and served on a bed of boiled potatoes and cherry tomatoes—a very subtle tasting and exquisite dish.

After eating, we finished our wine while enjoying the soft strains of the piano. It was a beautiful, relaxing evening.

Then I received the bill of one hundred euros. Maybe "Complimentary" had been the brand name of the champagne, not an offer.

At nine forty-five, feeling relaxed and fully stiffed—I mean stuffed—we walked back down through the nightclub to head home. The lounge was totally empty, except for a bartender. The crowds don't even start to go to these places until eleven, by which time we would have been asleep for an hour. I asked Joyce if she wanted to stop at the neon bar for a drink as a fitting ending to our stay. She softly squeezed my arm and said, "That's a lovely sentiment, but … at these prices? Are you crazy?" I guess Sharon Stone would have to wait until our next trip.

On Wednesday morning—October 13—we were to leave Positano and drive to Calabria. We woke to the heaviest rain since Tuscany. Up on the roof, breakfast was moved inside to a delightful room with windows on three sides. We took our time enjoying our last Punta Regina breakfast, sipping two cappuccinos. Joyce told Alessandro he made the best cappuccino in all of Italy, to which he gave a grand bow, the broadest smile, and a thank-you. We were celebrating the date. Today, Joyce's first Social Security check was being deposited into our bank account back home. We certainly needed it.

Upon entering the lobby, we were greeted by the ever-pleasant Tamara with, "Ah, Seniore and Seniora Gentile. The clouds are crying because you leave us today." How can a twenty something girl just pop poetry like that out of her mouth without thinking? I loved these people; I think their creativity is inborn. Perhaps living in such dramatic beauty affects one's sense of personal expression. I couldn't come up with a line like that if a thesaurus were surgically implanted in my brain. We immediately invited her to visit us if she ever went to America. She said she would love to. As I handed her my credit card, I calculated that if everyone on this trip we told to visit us actually did, we would have houseguests for the next thirty years. I honestly wouldn't mind any of them visiting.

Our sons were both married to wonderful women, so any future with Tamara was out of the question. But we had an unmarried daughter at home, and I was seriously thinking of whispering that sweet word into the ear of any number of these pleasant young men: "Green card." Well, maybe that's two words.

A Challenging Drive to Sicily

We had talked about seeing Paestium but decided to skip it because of the rain. We were eager to get some miles behind us as we headed for Sicily. I thought it would be nice to drive the Amalfi Road one last time. We could take it to Salerno before getting on the Autostrada A3 to Calabria. Midway between Amalfi and Salerno, we came behind one of those huge trucks one finds on the interstates back home, but rarely in Italy. The large rig didn't seem to belong on this narrow, winding road. Two cars served as the buffer between us and the truck, and eventually, about thirty cars had lined up behind us. We followed it for miles on the most treacherous parts of the road. It could barely negotiate the tight bends in the road and had to stop when an opposing vehicle approached. Then the two had to do a back-and-forth dance to get around each other.

We were really going very slowly for quite a while. The Italian drivers could take it no longer. They began to blow their horns—first a few, then more, then all of them. This cacophony of sounds in every pitch and tone imaginable created a deafening sound. But the truck just kept on trucking, and the drivers kept on honking. It was so outrageous that it gave us the giggles. Finally, at a straight stretch of road, the truck stopped and waved us on. All thirty drivers whooshed around the truck and us and were out of sight in seconds. Then, we passed.

Outside of Salerno, we finally entered A3, but it was different than the previous stretches of Autostrada. The road was now narrower and full of tight turns as it wound through Basilicata and into Calabria. Basilicata was densely forested. The mountains were steep, and wilderness pressed in all around. We saw no signs of towns or people, or even much traffic.

As we crossed Basilicata, a tremendous thunderstorm engulfed us. We had to slow down below 20 mph and drive with fog lights and flashers. It became foggy, and the rain was torrential. Visibility dropped to zero; it was a real panic ride, but there were no exits, and I didn't want to pull off the road in this godforsaken place, as long as I could keep moving—even at such a slow pace.

By the time the storm lifted, we were in Calabria. Poverty and neglect were evident; this locale was dramatically different from the Italy we had been enjoying. Where the grassy islands in the middle of the Autostrada had been beautifully planted and well kept throughout the rest of Italy, here they were overgrown and full of weeds. The road was in terrible shape, potholes and patches abounded, and some stretches were only two lanes wide. Road surfaces were uneven, and numerous construction signs were followed by half-completed sections, with no evidence of anyone working.

The distant hill towns did not look appealing; they appeared to be in disrepair, and in many cases looked deserted. No majestic church steeples or story book *castellos* adorned these places. Buildings seemed to be in ruin, with roofs partially collapsed and windows missing. Some even looked as if they had been gutted by fire. There were very few exits on this stretch of road, and when we saw one, there were no signs for hotels. We were getting tired and hungry. I wanted to stop for the night, but there didn't seem to be anyplace to do so—or at least not anywhere that looked safe.

It was after six and getting dark when another storm hit. Suddenly, I spotted an exit and veered onto it, thinking that if we followed the local road along the coast, we would come upon a seaside resort town and some hotels. Instead, we drove through what appeared to be slums and more derelict buildings. We passed stretches of ugly concrete apartment buildings, junkyards, cars that had been stripped and left along the roadside, and empty industrial buildings. Some looked as though they were under construction but had been abandoned before being completed. Even the people walking the streets looked frightening and unhappy. I told Joyce, "I'm getting back on the Autostrada. Even in the storms, I'll feel safer."

Miraculously, at the next entrance to the Autostrada, in the midst of several abandoned buildings and more junk, was the newly opened Grand Hotel Stella Maris. It was shiny and clean and had four stars. A double room was eighty-six euros, which included breakfast and a fenced-in parking court. It also had a restaurant, meaning we could stay in the safety of this oasis and take care of all our needs. It had a conference center, meeting rooms, and an indoor pool—none of which we needed, but welcomed none the less.

This hotel turned out to be part of a chain—one of those places that took in large groups on tour buses and served them awful food. Our meal, the worst of our trip, was a piece of shoe leather covered with a very strong, almost brown tomato sauce. This "cuisine" cost sixty-six euros, plus seven euros for a carafe of undrinkable wine. But the place was clean, and we and our car were safe. Dinner was served in a ballroom-sized dining room, big enough to handle those tour groups. There was only one other couple in the room, a couple from Germany. We exchanged pleasantries, but no conversation.

We were up early, endured an awful breakfast along with the German couple, and had embarked toward Sicily by nine thirty. Checking out of the hotel, I gave the desk clerk my Visa. She informed me it was rejected. Joyce and I figured the same block was put on mine that had been put on hers in Positano. We explained this to the desk clerk. She was not impressed. We paid with Joyce's Visa and were out of there. Don't get me wrong: it's not that the Calabrian countryside was ugly. It was beautiful. What man had done to it was ugly.

We had a quick and easy drive to Villa San Giovanni, a bustling port city with all the port-side industrialization you would expect: cranes, warehouses, trains, and acres of tracks. Villa San Giovanni is located at the tip of the toe of the boot, which is Italy, where it kicks the soccer ball that is Sicily. Since that gap represents the shortest distance between the mainland and the island, we chose it for our ferry ride. Directly across the water was Messina, one of Sicily's larger port cities and the closest to Taormina. We pulled up to a large terminal building fronted by a huge parking lot with painted lanes to a number of gates. I ran into the terminal and bought a round-trip ticket to Messina for thirty-five euros. The lanes were very well marked, and we got into the line for our ferry with just three cars in front of us. The very next car was that of the German couple; we smiled and waved.

Within ten minutes, the gates opened, and we were ushered onto a massive ferry the size of an oceangoing vessel. Metal ramps were connected to provide elevated bridgework for cars. Below, we could see buses and even a train going into the lower deck of the ferry. We parked, got out of the car, and walked to the rear deck to check out the scenery as the rest of the passengers boarded. The German couple left their car and walked to us. We talked about where we were going. They were going to Palermo. We told them we were going to Taormina. They asked where we were from and were surprised when we told them America. They thought we were British. Did we look sad as the ticket taker in Capri had observed? It must have been the look on our faces when we got our dinner at the hotel.

The port was extremely busy. Ferries were arriving and departing. Messina was a very short distance away and visible directly across from us. By nine thirty, we were pulling away from the dock. The ride would take twenty minutes. As we approached Messina, the view was pretty much the same as Villa San Giovanni: a heavily industrial seaport along the water with a fairly large city rising up the steep mountainside. A palm-lined boulevard ran along the water's edge, away from the port that seemed to be filled with hotels and a mix of old and modern buildings. It really didn't look like a place where we would want to linger.

The ferry glided effortlessly into its slip, and rather quickly, we were guided off and into the fray of this busy port city. We zigzagged through a warren of confusing streets, but the signage was very good, and in no time, we were out of town and merging onto Autostrada A18. I secretly hoped the signage going the opposite direction was as good; then I would easily be able to find my way back to the ferry when the time came.

Total Relaxation at Taormina

Sicily was beautiful, and the drive to Taormina was very pleasant. The country-side was mountainous and arid; the soil was rocky, with bits of scrub brush cling-ing to rock faces. Palms and cacti abounded. Flowers bloomed everywhere in the steamy mid-October heat. As we sped along the Autostrada, with mountains of stone on our right and the sea on our left, a hot haze shrouded the coast, making the nearby mainland invisible.

Taormina was built on the cliff tops overlooking the sea and was connected to the beach below by a funicular. A18 tunneled under the town; we exited just before the tunnel. Once we had exited the Autostrada, we rode to town on a nar-row, winding road that made a serpentine climb up this rocky ledge. The streets of town were the narrow, medieval lanes we had become accustomed to—so nar-row we had to, once again, pull in our side mirrors. Many of the streets were pedestrian only, except for local deliveries. We found ourselves circling through them a few times before finally finding our bed and breakfast.

The Hotel La Pensione Svizzera was a delightful little pink stucco place that clung precariously to the hillside to achieve a great view of the sea. Owned and operated by the Vinciguerra family since 1925, the three-star hotel had twenty-two rooms on four floors, along with limited parking that could be reserved in advance for eight euros a day. There was no elevator, and we had the pleasure of a room with a terrace overlooking the sea on the top floor. The idea was appealing. The reality was seventy-eight steps that became the ultimate stress test as I strug-gled to carry our luggage up, then hauled myself up and down at least four times a day. But once up top and in our very small and modest room, we enjoyed the lovely terrace, the dramatic view, many glasses of wine, and occasional CPR.

The streets of this town were very congested—packed with tourists enjoying the autumn sun and heat. The drivers were even crazier than those on the Amalfi Drive. I was happy I had reserved a parking space. The owner gave me a key to my parking space and explained it was the third one behind the hotel. Joyce and I left our bags in the lobby and went to park the car. After half an hour, a number of trips around the hotel, and several attempts to unlock various garage doors with that key, I ran back in to clarify just where this parking space was to be found.

Smiling at my stupidity, he explained there were four metal poles on the road-side behind the hotel, each connected by a length of chain that was padlocked to the poles. The key would unlock the third length of chain, and then I could park in between those two poles. It was that simple. Except those poles were spaced the exact length of my car and about a foot out from the building. So as Joyce tried to signal the buses, cars, and scooters that roared past while honking their horns, I sweated to squeeze the car into a space smaller than the car itself, tapping the poles with each move until I actually did it. Climbing out the passenger door, I surveyed my eight-euro-a-day target for every vehicle careening down this narrow alley, then went inside to shower and resuscitate myself.

We decided to take a walk to get a feel for the area. Taormina had an interesting layout for a seaside resort town. Down along the water's edge, a road meandered along the irregular shoreline. It was dotted with resort hotels, taverns, restaurants, and private homes tightly squeezed into little slips of steeply sloping land between the road and the sea. The scalloped edge of the cliff-laden coast created tiny crescents of beach interrupted by rocky outcroppings housing sumptuous private villas. This tight, congested chunk of land between water and cliff was loaded with small patches of beach dotted with little thatch-roofed umbrellas, beach chairs, and outdoor cafés. People in swimsuits and sandals walked, sunned, ate, and drank, just enjoying the beach and sun in a very casual atmosphere. Far above, running along a ridge halfway up the mountain side, was a bustling town—rich and sophisticated, with streets lined with shops and churches and villas. Smartly dressed people, antique shops, and restaurants all vied for attention in a city that bore no resemblance to a seaside resort. Far above this scene, a medieval village topped by a fortress reigned supreme, with views of the vast world beyond. None of these very different environments seemed to acknowledge the other.

A short walk up our street took us to Corso Umberto, Taormina's main street. This mile-long, very wide, pedestrian-only, cobbled boulevard was lined with trendy shops selling everything from Nikes and cell phones to haute couture. Beautiful old villas had been converted into expensive antique galleries, restaurants, and hotels. Each end of the boulevard was defined by a massive arch seemingly left from the gate of a fortress wall long gone. Narrow side streets filled with shops and restaurants jutted out from either side of Corso Umberto. On the one side, they climbed the steep hillside, revealing palm trees and lush gardens of homes terraced up above the town; on the other side, the lanes dropped toward the cliff edge, giving glimpses of the sea below and beyond.

All these streets were filled with nicely dressed people strolling in and out of the shops, chatting, eating gelato, or just browsing. We joined in the parade. This was truly a vibrant town, filled with an international but also very heavily Italian crowd, leading me to believe this was a very popular Italian vacation spot.

We stopped for lunch at an enchanting little garden café appropriately called A Fammara Giardino, tucked away off a narrow side street and set on a terrace under a stand of orange trees. This establishment advertised true old Sicilian recipes, and the meal did not disappoint. Sicily has been occupied by so many cultures that its cuisine is different than the rest of Italy. It is a fusion of French, African, Greek, and Italian, resulting in some unusual and very delicious dishes.

After our meal, we continued our exploration of the town. Taormina's main square was Piazza 9 Aprile. It was a wide open patio with a stone floor set in a diamond pattern, with Corso Umberto running right through it and majestic buildings on three sides. On the fourth side, an iron-railed overlook cantilevered out over a cliff that plummeted to the sea below. The magnificent view from there included the water, shoreline, and threatening Mount Etna spewing steam in the rather near distance. As we approached 9 Aprile, a wedding party was leaving the church that fronted the piazza, Chiesa di San Giuseppe. The hill shot up behind the church, and a waterfall surrounded by flowers cascaded down one side. The railings of the terrace outside the church doors and the stairs were decorated with yellow apples cut in half and pinned to a garland of lemon leaves. The effect was really beautiful.

Feeling a bit tired, we returned to our hotel to relax on our terrace, read, and sip the remainder of our limoncello from Positano.

Our terrace was a gem. We had a 360-degree view of the world. The haze had lifted, and we could look straight out across the water to the tip of the toe of mainland Italy. To the left was the irregular Sicilian shoreline, creating tiny crescents of beach and an occasional rock promontory that barely concealed a stone villa covered with tropical vegetation. The funicular carried tourists to the beach below, gliding past so close that we could see the passengers' faces. To our right, the Moorish style peaked arches and flat, notched roofs of hotels and houses were wedged into the hillside, with flowering plants spilling over their terraces. Above them all was a peek at the outer wall of the second century BC Greco-Roman theater. Behind us, the rocky terrain raised dramatically to the crow's-nest village of Castelmola and its imposing fortress walls.

I was in sensory overload. My eyes struggled to absorb the sight of these uniquely different buildings; palms; cacti; cypress, lemon, and orange trees; massive terra-cotta pots filled with flowers; and walls dripping with vines. This vision combined with the sweet smell of the explosion of flowers and flowering plants, along with a rainbow of laundry hanging from rooftop lines. I could close my eyes and hear the heartbeat of this vibrant town: people chattering and laughing; buses, cars, and Vespas zooming by; the soft purr of the funicular; dogs barking; birds chirping; children playing; and, in the distance, music. If I concentrated really hard, I could even hear the sea washing up against the rocky shore. Up above it all, I drifted on a limoncello-spiked cloud.

I hated to break the spell, but it was time for *passeggiata*. We changed into nicer clothes, getting into the custom, and walked the length of Corso Umberto, stopping in a few shops along the way. After nearly a month of massive meals, we were beginning to feel overstuffed. It seemed a wise decision to cut back and start eating lightly, so that we would be able to fit into the seats for the flight home. We stopped at a little trattoria and, sitting at a front-row table, we sipped wine and ate bruschetta with tomatoes, speck ham, and artichoke while watching the parade of people passing by. After nearly two hours of this strenuous activity, it was time to get up from our table and walk back to the hotel for a sound night's sleep.

On Friday, we thought we'd take a tour of Mount Etna. Etna is Europe's largest active volcano, and, after the Alpine peaks, the 11,032-foot mountain is the highest in Italy. There have been over a hundred known eruptions of Etna, and major activity occurs in intervals of four to twelve years. The most recent eruption was in August of 2001. This summer, scientists and photographers were studying some very colorful activity of that great cauldron. I found that little bit of news somewhat unsettling. But she did not disappoint; Etna was glowing beautifully.

A number of tour offices along the street advertised trips to Etna and, after breakfast in our lush little garden, we took a walk to one of them. These tours left at 7:00 AM; we were too late for a tour that day. We asked to book one for tomorrow and were told they did not go to Etna on Saturdays, but it was possible to go ourselves. The tour lady told us it was a one and a half hour drive to a village where it would be possible to hire a jeep that could only take us to a spot two thousand feet below the crater. The tram that went to the top had been destroyed in the 2001 activity of the volcano, and no one was allowed any nearer. We dreaded the thought of three hours in the car and felt there probably was a better view of Etna from Piazza 9 Aprile than two thousand feet under its rim, so we scratched the idea of an Etna trip.

Instead, we walked to the Greco-Roman theater and had a great experience. It was moving to walk through this antiquity, and the views were enthralling. On such a crystal-clear day, it seemed Etna was spewing steam and lava just for us. We took photos and listened to a talk about the history of the theater, then headed for the funicular and lunch at a trattoria on the beach. It was charming in a tacky sort of way, and we decided to rent chaises the next day and have a beach day. For now, it was time to return to the hotel, drink a little limoncello, and siesta. To our horror, we found the limoncello bottle was empty.

I decided I would call Visa and clear up my hold when we took *passeggiata*. I still had time on my Italian calling card. I must have spent half an hour at a pay phone on the street, trying to get the calling card to work internationally and getting through to the correct person at Visa. Very frustrated and angry, I finally cleared it up, and the security hold was lifted from my Visa.

If I hadn't needed more limoncello before, I certainly needed that tranquilizer now. To our pleasant surprise, we found a shop that was hosting a complimentary tasting. We tried an orangecello that was heavenly. The taste was far deeper and richer than limoncello; we were hooked. New bottles of orangecello in each hand, we headed for the hotel and some chill time.

That evening, I was awakened by a powerful thunderstorm. I like to sleep through a storm; I hate to get awakened in the middle of the night, because I start to obsess over things and can't fall back to sleep. I started obsessing about the drive back to Venice. What if we encountered another storm like the one we had encountered on the drive down? I should have listened to Joyce and turned the car in at Taormina, then gotten the train to Venice. Was there still time to make that change? And so it went through the night.

It was still raining in the morning, so we had breakfast inside. By the time we finished with breakfast, the rain had stopped, the sun was out and—immediately—everything was dry. It was a short walk to the funicular for our ride to the beach. While we stood in a line of about ten people, two American couples walked into the station, talking very loudly, and walked past everyone in line to "look out the windows at the view." When the funicular pulled in, the two couples never took a break in their loud talking and simply walked in front of everyone and onto the funicular. A group of Germans who had been next to us in line got into our car. The man in the group looked at the couples in the car in front of us and said, in English, "Americans—it's no wonder everyone hates them." I thought he must have said that in English for our benefit, but how could I respond? These particular Americans were rude, but not all Americans. I let it go and concentrated on the beach.

For five euros each, we rented two beach chairs and positioned ourselves for some sun and relaxation. My worries of the night before had completely dissolved. The drive to Venice would be a piece of cake. Hadn't I driven from our place in Pittsburgh to the beach at South Carolina in one day a hundred times? Why would this be any different? It was about the same distance. I had made the beach in twelve hours, and I could do this in about the same amount of time. I would cruise along my favorite road, the Autostrada, the whole way. What could possibly go wrong?

Two young Vietnamese girls walked the beach, offering full body massages with oil, right there at our beach chairs, for fifteen euros for a half hour. Joyce decided to have one and said it was great. She told me to have one. I had never had a massage. I was reluctant; I wasn't sure if this was legal. Who was I kidding? This was Sicily. Sure, I'd have one. It was great. I was hooked. I felt so good that I once again had to wonder if I had just broken the law. I felt like a rag doll. I didn't think my legs would carry me, but we walked up to the patio of the Ristoranti il Baracailo for lunch.

To get to Ristoranti il Baracailo, we had to get out of our chaises, which was quite an effort after the massage. Then we had to walk along a narrow sidewalk that hugged the edge of a stone wall that seemed to be there to keep the narrow lawn of the hotel from slipping into the sea. Once past the hotel, we walked by little bungalows—the homes of fishing families. The fishermen sat outside them, mending their nets. They nodded and offered a "*Boun giorno*" as we passed and continued up the stone stairs that served as these people's street from their homes to the main road above. The restaurant was midway up the stairs; the building, housing indoor seating and the kitchen, was nestled into the hillside, and a vine-covered patio for outside seating was terraced over the water. This patio was fitted tightly between lemon trees and garden herbs, and under ancient vines on the brink of teetering over the cliff's edge.

Time seemed to stop as we reveled in this most delightful relaxed setting and enjoyed another great meal. We had fresh pasta with swordfish, tomatoes, and zucchini that I am certain came from the garden surrounding us. A couple from our hotel and a couple we had been on the funicular with were eating there. They joined us in pleasant conversation. It was amazing to me how often we saw the same people several times as we traveled, and that the camaraderie was so freely felt and offered.

In the evening, we attended mass at San Giuseppe. A man and woman were celebrating their fiftieth wedding anniversary, and the church was full of relatives and friends. Everyone in church was made part of the celebration. Afterward, we took a table at a very nice wine bar on the piazza. They say Piazza 9 Aprile is Taormina's living room, and it is true. Elderly people sat on the benches talking, and younger couples conversed as their children played soccer in the middle of the piazza. That was perhaps a little too homey for me, as we had to dodge a few errant balls. But I was impressed with how indulgent the Italian parents were with their children, and no one but me seemed to mind these flying missiles.

It was dark, and molten lava ran down the side of Etna, as if the giant hand of God had cracked open a soft-boiled egg, pouring out its yolk. Joyce and I were amazed that Etna was that active. I secretly hoped it would wait at least one more day—until we were back on the mainland—before blowing its top. We saw the couple from Ireland that had been on our boat to Capri and had a pleasant conversation with them.

We bought an orange made of mascarpone, a very popular confection beautifully displayed in shop windows all over Taormina, and walked back to the room for an early night. We were planning to be up at the crack of dawn for the drive to Venice. Back in the room, we put the TV on the BBC channel. There was a special on the sex issue of the election; I hadn't even known there was one. The show was coming from Pittsburgh, and we knew one of the speakers. It was a strange feeling to be sitting in a room in Sicily, watching someone we knew talking on a television show back in Pittsburgh about the presidential election.

On our way into the hotel, we encountered a group of people from Germany who were checking in. They had two rooms on our floor and two rooms on other floors. They were the loudest, noisiest people I have ever heard. They banged doors, yelled from room to room, and even shouted from our floor to those on floors below. The racket continued past midnight on the one night we wanted a good night's sleep. I could only think of the outrage of the Germans on the funicular and how the Americans' lack of consideration for others paled compared to this.

Another Harrowing Drive

Wanting to get an early start, we asked for a 5:00 AM wake-up call, but set our alarm as a safety measure. It's a good thing we did, because the call never came. We awakened to the alarm and walked out onto the terrace. It was a beautiful morning; the sky was loaded with more stars than I have ever seen. Standing for a while arm in arm, we were feeling a little melancholy, reluctant to leave. We grabbed our bags and started down the seventy-eight stairs for the last time. I was tempted to bang my suitcases all the way down for our German friends, but my bags held too many fragile items. (But I must admit, I closed my door a little loudly.) The night man who was to give us our wake-up call was sound asleep, in his underwear, on a cot in the middle of the tiny lobby. He slowly got up, casually offered us breakfast as he walked to the bar, made cappuccinos, handed them to us with juice and great pastries, then climbed back into his cot.

After eating, we quietly walked past him on our way to the car. He raised his head, asked us to be certain to lock the door, and went back to sleep.

The drive to Messina was tranquil as the sun rose through an early morning mist. I was feeling that peace one feels early in the morning before others are awake; the sunrise felt fresh, the air held a faint dewy smell, and the world seemed clean and young. The route back to the ferry was well marked, and we seemed to navigate it in no time. After only a twenty-minute wait, we boarded the ferry, and not long after, the vessel quickly and smoothly departed. When we arrived on the mainland at Villa san Giovanni at 8:00 AM, disembarkation was quick and easy. But all of that was about the extent of the peace and calm we would enjoy that day.

Effortlessly, I drove off the ferry and straight onto the Autostrada. The drive through Calabria was fine. There was the expected slowdown when the road went from four lanes to two through stretches of construction—or stretches marked for construction, anyway—where, hopefully, Calabria would one day have an Autostrada that resembled the rest of Italy's, but the ride was not bad. Then, as we were going through the rugged mountains where Calabria meets Basilicata, another thunderstorm hit. Before long, though, we were out of it. I thought I was making good time.

Outside of Salerno, we screeched to a halt and spent forty-five minutes merging from four lanes into one, thanks to more construction. Still, it wasn't that bad; not too many trucks were on the road. The man at the hotel had told us trucks were not allowed on the Autostrada on Sundays. In one of our travel guides, Joyce had read that decals were issued to trucks; these permits staggered the days each vehicle was permitted on the Autostrada. That way, not all of them would be traveling at the same time. We figured from the number of trucks on the road, there must have been a decal for Sundays. We definitely saw more trucks on the Autostrada than on previous trips to Italy.

We managed to get through the congestion around Naples and Rome well enough, only stopping to photograph the Abbey at Montecassino from the highway. The abbey had been founded by St. Benedict in 529. The village and hills around it had been occupied by the Germans in the Second World War, and this was the site of one of the bitterest and most controversial battles of that war. In the five months before the Allies managed to take possession, the abbey had been bombed to the ground, and 54,000 members of the Allied forces, and 20,000 of the German forces had lost their lives. The abbey had since been rebuilt, and I had wanted to see it, but had scrapped the plan because of the lack of time. So we had to be content seeing it from the distance of the Autostrada.

Once in Tuscany, I felt back at home, and was beginning to feel relaxed; then we were stopped for nearly an hour. We expected to pass an accident, only to find it was, once again, construction. This happened again at Florence, which perplexed me, because we had not seen any construction outside of Calabria before that day. That led me to believe the Italians must work on the Autostrada on Sundays, because it was supposed to be the lightest travel day. I didn't think that Sundays could be considered light any longer!

I was tired, cranky, and hungry. In the mountains of Emilia Romagna, I pulled off into one of the roadside rest areas. It had been our experience that these places served good food—far better than our roadside places on America's interstates—and they also had self-serve wine dispensers. I knew this might be the last rest area we would pass before stopping for the night, and I really needed some wine.

A number of tour buses and tons of cars were parked in the area, but we felt all these people could easily be accommodated by the array of choices, from food-to-go, and stand-up bars to full cafeterias, so we went into the cafeteria and got some excellent gnocchi with pesto and a carafe of wine for pennies. While we were eating, more tour buses pulled in, and the place became a mob scene: about a hundred ladies fought for a place in line for the restroom, and the men ravaged the wine dispensers. A line formed out the door for the cash register, and everyone was shouting and pushing. It was worse than a basement sale at Macy's.

We quickly got out of there. On the way out, I counted twelve tour busses in the parking lot. No wonder the place was crazy; everyone was trying to take care of all their bodily needs in the ten minutes allowed by these tour packages.

I did not feel refreshed from that stop and would have liked to get a room for the night, but there was nothing around. We kept driving. Crossing Italy, Joyce and I had marveled at the number of tunnels on the Autostrada. Upon setting out from Taormina, we decided to pass the time counting the tunnels from Villa San Giovanni to Venice. Every time we entered one, I would say the number in Italian, and Joyce would repeat it in English. It was cute the first ten hours, but by the time we leveled into the flatlands around Bologna and endured another half hour construction delay, we had counted 138 tunnels, somehow breaking the mood in the process.

I desperately wanted to find a room for the night. Suddenly, I noticed how ugly the land was—long, flat stretches of nothing broken only by an occasional industrial site. Why hadn't I noticed this on the last trip to Venice? There were no signs for hotels, and the exits looked very desolate—even a bit dangerous. Stark, massive mills loomed in fields. I wasn't going to risk wasting time or compromising our safety by taking these exits just to look for something. My eyes were out of focus and on fire, I felt as though someone were driving an iron stake through my skull, someone else was playing the Anvil Chorus on timpani in my head, my ears were ringing, and my back ached. I was in a foul mood, and so was Joyce.

Suddenly, a lone sign for a hotel emerged. We took the exit and paid our toll. A hundred yards away, in the middle of a barren field, sat a building—the only building—and a welcoming sign that identified the structure as Hotel Savonarola. It was newly built, ostensibly for business travel: sterile, with no character. I didn't care, it was a wonderful sight. Our room cost one hundred and four euros for the night; it could have cost a thousand, and we would have taken it. I immediately dove into bed. In the morning, after an uneventful breakfast, we were back on the road, and within an hour, we were parking our car in Venice, along a sidewalk at Piazzale Roma, directly in front of the Auto Europe office.

Nostalgic and Romantic Last Day in Venice

The car drop was really easy. As we were unloading our luggage, a man came out of the office, handed me a receipt, and drove the car away. We walked across the street, down a ramp between two buildings, and found ourselves standing in the bright sun on the edge of the Grand Canal, right across from the train station. There before us was our old friend Venice, with all its clamor and glorious beauty.

We were staying at La Locanda di Orsaria, which was an eight-minute walk from the piazzale—honest! (It said so right there in the brochure.) We started to walk, carrying all our worldly possessions—which had grown considerably since arriving in Italy, especially in weight. It was necessary to cross three bridges, which included steps up and back down to get over the canals. The bridge over the Grand Canal was especially high. Joyce had a carry-on, a shopping bag full of loot, and her purse. I had the big suitcase with our second carry-on laced to the top of it. A thick bag we had bought in Sicily to fit all of our new acquisitions into was over my shoulder, along with my camera bag. It was warm for late October in Venice, at least to me. In the half hour that it took us to reach the hotel, I had lost a considerable number of pounds through perspiration and had seriously—possibly permanently—damaged the wrist and elbow of my right arm.

It was before noon, and the room was not ready, so we left everything with the front-desk person and went out to enjoy our bonus of one more full day in Venice. The weather had changed since our last visit three weeks ago. We were still comfortable in our shirtsleeves, but the locals wore jackets or sweaters and sported scarves rakishly knotted around their necks. The Italians seemed a very stylish people in their dress—more so than the French—and the Venetians added even more flair to their wardrobes than the rest of Italy.

Our hotel was in a tiny alley around the corner from the train station. We walked on the station side of the Grand Canal through unfamiliar territory: along Rio Terra di Spagna, then Rio Terra S. Leonardo and Via V Emanuelle and Strada Nouva, a network of the broadest shop-lined streets in Venice, until reaching the familiar Rialto, and on through the labyrinth of tiny shop-lined alleys to St. Mark's Square and back. Along the way, we walked through the Jewish ghetto—the first in all of Europe. It was chock-full of small ethnic shops and kosher delis and boasted a very active produce market. We stopped at a tiny trattoria for a delicious, light lunch. We thought we saw Madame X talking to the butcher in one of the kosher delis, but didn't approach her for fear she would scold us for leaving our towels on the floor when we checked out.

Back at the hotel, we transferred all of our luggage to our room and freshened up for the evening. I added my sport coat to my jeans and polo shirt, and Joyce donned the new scarf she had bought on our walk. She tied it around her neck into a jaunty knot in the style of the locals. Feeling very Venetian, we headed out for the evening.

Passing through Campo St. Geremia on our earlier walk, I had noticed an interesting-looking church that, for some reason, I wanted to see more closely. I read the plaque: Chiesa dei Santi Geremia e Lucia. Inside was a huge side altar topped by a glass sarcophagus. Elaborate candelabras holding candles in red glass lanterns surrounded it, and a tiny woman lay inside. It was possible to walk behind the altar and all around this person. She was dressed in a beautifully embroidered red and gold gown, but no shoes. Her hands and feet were blackened but intact, the skin still on. She had never decomposed, but her face and head were covered with a gold mask.

I picked up a brochure and read this was Santa Lucia, born in Sicily in the third century, martyred by being beheaded at the age of twenty-three. Her followers hid her body and head in catacombs to keep the Romans from destroying them, and through the centuries, they had been moved several times, going as far as Constantinople. Finally, her body had come to this final resting place in Venice. She became known as the patron saint of the blind. It finally hit us: this was Saint Lucy, patron saint of the blind and namesake of the Medallion Ball in Pittsburgh, a charity debutant ball in which our daughter had been a participant. We never even knew Lucy was in Venice, and now we had stood mere feet away from her—another bonus on this trip loaded with surprises and unforgettable experiences.

Back outside, the sun was getting low. We walked to St. Mark's Square and got a table at Quadri, one of the outrageously expensive cafés lining the perimeter of the square. This one, founded in 1638 and frequented by Wagner, featured a string orchestra that serenaded its guests and competed with the orchestra at its rival café across the square, Café Florian, which had been established in 1720 and frequented by Lord Byron and Casanova. We had decided to forgo the flashy notoriety of Florian and go to the quieter, older guy on the block.

As we took our seats, I noticed the waiters, who wore white dinner jackets and black ties. They stood clustered in casual conversation, fairly oblivious to us. One of them reluctantly drew himself away from the conversation to walk over. Through slightly elevated and flared nostrils, he informed us that before we got comfortable, we should know that the table charge was two euros per person, and an orchestra cover charge of 2.4 euros per person was tacked onto every order as well. I smiled and said that would be fine. He returned my smile in a painful, constipated sort of way and asked what we would like. I asked for two proseccos, and he was gone as quickly as he came.

It was an evening right out of a Fellini film: the setting sun cast long shadows of the Campanile across the square; the mosaics on the face of St. Marks glistened in the dying light; and the chimes rang and sent the pigeons fluttering and swooping through the square as tourists walked about with outstretched handfuls of feed. The orchestra was softly playing a medley of Italian love songs, and the waiter had just set a pewter tray covered with a white linen cloth at our table. It held a tiny dish of nuts and two shimmering flutes of frosty prosecco. When our orchestra would stop playing, the orchestra at Florian's would start, and so went the evening washed in soft light, string music, and sweet, chilled prosecco.

We were in Venice, enjoying our last night of the romantic, lush, magical sweetness that was Italy. We were more relaxed than we had been in years. I was happy. I was in love. I could have stayed there with Joyce, our prosecco, and the music forever.

But we had to be up at three thirty in the morning to make our flight. I reluctantly signaled the waiter and was immediately catapulted back to reality when he presented me with our twenty-four-euro check. We strolled out of the square hand in hand, stopping along our walk back to the hotel for a piece of pizza, and again for one last great dessert, which we took back to the room and had with the last of our orangecello.

I had a fitful night's sleep. For some time, I had been secretly worried about the two of us walking alone down deserted alleys at four in the morning, carrying all our bags in total darkness. Through the night, I would awaken in a sweat with visions of us being followed, brutally attacked, and thrown into the canal as the villains departed with all our worldly belongings. We had asked at the desk about the safety of walking to the bus stop that early in the morning. Our desk man had just shrugged and said, "In Venice is no danger. Not to worry." Somehow, that did not reassure.

However, once we got outside, we found that the area was well lit, and a surprising amount of people walked briskly about. Many seemed to be on their way to work; others were tourists—mostly kids with backpacks just arriving or leaving. It was very safe and, except for the total destruction of my wrist from carrying everything back over the bridges, uneventful. We arrived at the bus stop with ten minutes to spare.

The Flight Home and Reflections of a Life-Changing Experience

Lines were already forming at the airport, despite the early hour. It seemed everyone leaving Venice had a 6:00 AM flight. One couple in front of us looked very irritated. They were taking an excessive amount of time checking in. They were Americans—and, I imagined, were headed for our flight. These two were loaded to the ceiling with an extravagant pile of luggage, which apparently didn't guarantee happiness. They were arguing with the person at the counter and each other. It seemed they were way over on the allowed baggage weight and arguing about the fees to be paid. They were also disagreeing over who had the passports and who had the tickets and who was dumber for not knowing where things were or were not. As the woman rummaged through her bags, one of those cheesy (and very expensive) souvenir wine glasses fell out and broke on the floor. Her husband berated her.

Suddenly, the man cursed loudly, searching for his wallet. They both started going through their luggage, tearing things apart until he made the exclamation that he had left his wallet with money, credit cards, and ID under his pillow at the hotel. He jumped onto his cell phone and barked orders to someone at the hotel. Meanwhile, his wife was triumphantly proclaiming him the dumber of the two in between sobs of, "What are we going to do?" Barely concealing their glee, the counter people told them they would have to step aside, and we were processed in their place.

We got through check-in and boarded the plane without a hitch, never to see the troubled couple again. But I couldn't help but think of the stereotypical ugly American and contrast that notion with the laid-back, simplistic logic we had encountered throughout this trip. I hoped I would never become as self-absorbed as those poor representations of American ostentation.

The flight was smooth and relaxing. There was a four-hour layover in Frankfurt, but we would enjoy the comforts of the first-class lounge. Security was so tight in Frankfurt that our stay in the lounge was reduced to two hours by the time we got through, but they were pleasant hours. Drinking cappuccino and eating pastries, we read *USA Today* and the *New York Times* from cover to cover. As we got back into English-speaking mode and updated ourselves on the pre-election battle, we were so very at ease. We started talking about the kids and our mothers, planning what we would do upon arrival in Pittsburgh. It seemed we had been gone long enough. Joyce wondered if her plants were still alive. I wondered if Heather would be at the airport to meet us. We were switching mental gears from dreamland to reality, but not too quickly.

We walked leisurely to the gate, boarded the plane, and graciously received the ultimate pampering of first class. The treatment started with mimosas, then went to wine. A gourmet meal was served on china, followed by fruit, cheese, dessert, and an after-dinner drink. After that, we watched a movie. We watched *DeLovely*, the story of Cole Porter, and enjoyed the story and music. After the movie, snacks were served. I switched my headset to an album of Henry Mancini music, closed my eyes, and thought about our adventures of the past month.

This had truly been the experience of a lifetime. We had immersed ourselves in the culture, acquired some great Italian recipes, met wonderful people, and learned so much more. I met my family and gained a greater understanding of my father. We had felt guilty about retiring and had been agitated and stressed when we left home; now we were very relaxed, mellow, and happy. The trip had transformed us.

Travel can be broadening and mood altering, but often the obvious benefits of relaxation and renewal are temporary. But this time, something told me this feeling would last. Our attitudes had changed in so many ways. We could never be the same. Sure, by the time we left the airport parking lot, we would be smacking into the same frustrations and obligations that were there when we left, but maybe, just maybe, we would face them with a renewed spirit and vigor. Hopefully, they would not control us or consume our thoughts, as they had before we left on our trip. We had grown through our experiences—and grown closer together.

I drifted in and out of Mancini's music and felt the most wonderful peace and calm. I told Joyce to tune into the music. "Two for the Road" was playing. I had never thought about it before, but now, for the first time, I realized the words to this song had a great deal of meaning for us and our life together. Joyce and I toasted with our wine and kissed. For a month, we had spent twenty-four hours a day together and enjoyed every minute of it; we had reconnected and reaffirmed our love for each other, and we were now closer than ever. Holding hands and resting our heads on our pillows with our eyes closed, we let the song softly lead us through the wonders of the past month: the delectable smells and tastes of the *fattoria* and our cooking classes; the charm of the warm and tender people; peaceful walks through the country; the beauty and piety of Padua and Assisi; the adventure and drama of the Amalfi Coast and contentment of Positano; the serenity of the tiny Tuscan, Umbrian, and Abruzesse hill towns; the joy of connecting with family; the relaxation of Taormina; and the mysterious, seductive romance of Venice.

"Moon River" was playing again, just as it had on our flight to Italy. Much had changed since then. We squeezed hands without opening our eyes.

It was forty years ago, and we were dancing to this very song on our wedding day. "Moon River, wider than a mile, I'm crossing you in style someday ..." And we had. We had been young and in love and full of dreams and hopes for the future back then. Now we had realized many of our dreams—and even surpassed some. But even as we traveled, we had made new plans and dreamed new dreams. We enjoyed forty wonderful years together, had three loving and caring children and two great daughters-in-law, endured few problems, and shared countless blessings and experiences. We had enjoyed every minute of our lives together and were still looking forward to each new day.

Retirement was not the end. There was much more we had to do, and I was so looking forward to it. "Two drifters, off to see the world, there's such a lot of world to see."

And there is ... there certainly is.

"Twenty years from now you will be more disappointed by the things you didn't do than by the ones you did do. So throw off the bowlines. Sail away from the safe harbor. Catch the trade winds in your sails. Explore. Dream. Discover."

—Mark Twain

Recipes

Duck Sauce

1 3/4 pounds duck breast
3 carrots, chopped
3 stocks of celery, chopped
2 small red onions, quartered
3 cloves garlic
1 cup olive oil
1 cup dry, red wine
3 tbsp tomato paste
1 tsp fennel seeds
salt and pepper to taste

- Trim fat off duck breast and run it through a meat grinder.

- Spread it on a cookie sheet and bake in a preheated oven at 300 degrees Fahrenheit for ten minutes.

- Run carrots, celery, onions, and garlic through meat grinder.

- Add olive oil to the mixture, then add salt and pepper to taste.

- Sauté mixture in a large pot over medium-high heat for 5 minutes.

- Drain fat from duck and add to vegetable mixture. Cook for 2 to 3 minutes, stirring all the time to avoid burning.

- Once mixture is dry, add the cup of wine and let it reduce slightly. Add tomato paste, and reduce heat to simmer.

- Add fennel seeds.

- Cover mixture with water and simmer for 1½ hours uncovered.

- If sauce is dry, stir in a cup of water.

Fresh Pasta

Makes 6 servings

3 cups all-purpose flour
4 eggs
1 tbsp olive oil
1 tsp salt
water

- Break eggs into a mixing bowl.

- Add olive oil and a pinch of salt.

- Gradually add flour and mix all together—first by fork, then by hand as consistency becomes tight.

- Knead dough on countertop, adding additional flour if needed until dough is shiny and springs back slightly when you press your finger into the top.

- Shape dough into loaf, wrap with plastic wrap, and refrigerate for ½ hour.

- Lightly flour countertop. Cut dough into ½-inch slices and run through flattening rollers of pasta machine.

- Pass each slice through the machine twice at each setting, changing from thick to thin settings. Sprinkle flour onto dough if needed to avoid stickiness.

- After all slices are flattened, change to cutting roll on the machine. Cut all slices and spread on a floured baking sheet or drying rack to dry.

- Bring a large pot of salted water to a boil.

- Drop noodles into the pot and cook for 6 minutes or until they are al dente.

Gnudi

Makes 6 servings and is an excellent side to any veal dish

24-ounce container of ricotta (sheep if possible, cow if not)
2 cups fresh-grated Parmesan cheese
2 10-ounce boxes frozen chopped spinach
3 large eggs
1/2 tsp fresh nutmeg
1/2 tsp salt
1/2 tsp pepper
2/3 cup all-purpose flour
olive oil
truffle oil

- Thaw, drain, and squeeze all water out of the spinach.

- In a large bowl, mix ricotta, parmesan cheese, spinach, yolks of 2 eggs, and 1 whole egg.

- Grate nutmeg into the mixture.

- Add salt, pepper, and flour.

- Mix all ingredients together by hand.

- Bring large pot of salted water to a boil.

- Put mixture into a pastry bag. Squeeze dough out of bag, cutting off 1-inch pieces into the boiling water. Dough may be rolled into little balls if no pastry bag is available.

- Cook for a few minutes until they float to the surface of the water, then scoop them out and drop them into an ice bath.

- Divide gnudi into six individual oven-safe baking bowls that have been lightly greased with olive oil.

- Sprinkle with parmesan cheese and pepper.

- Bake uncovered at 375 degrees for 15 minutes.

- Drizzle lightly with truffle oil and serve.

Crema di Ceci (cream of chickpea soup)

Makes 8 servings

4 strips of pancetta or bacon, chopped
11 cloves garlic, minced
3 sprigs fresh rosemary, off stems and roughly chopped
1/2 tsp red pepper flakes
6 16-ounce cans of chickpeas with liquid
2 tsp tomato paste
1/2 cup white wine
2 tsp olive oil
salt and pepper

- In a large, heavy pot, sauté the chopped bacon in the olive oil. Add garlic, rosemary, and pepper flakes. Continue to sauté on medium heat until garlic is lightly golden. Be careful not to burn the garlic.

- Add chickpeas with liquid to the pot, along with tomato paste and wine; bring to a boil, then simmer uncovered over medium-low heat for ½ hour, stirring occasionally.

- When mixture has cooled slightly, run it through a blender or food processor and return to the pot.

- Add one cup of water, then salt and pepper to taste. Simmer for 5 minutes.

- Serve in soup bowls. Garnish with fried squid ink angel hair noodles (see following recipe).

Fried Squid-Ink Angel Hair

1/4 lb. squid-ink angel hair (may substitute spinach or any dark herb angel hair)
1 1/2 cups sunflower oil

- Cook pasta in large pot of boiling water until al dente and quickly remove.

- In a small pot, bring oil to a boil.

- Drop a small handful of the noodles into the oil and fry briefly.

- Remove with slotted spoon and set on paper towels to drain.

- Repeat for amount of noodles desired.

- Garnish soup with fried noodles.

De Medici Salad

Makes 8 servings

1-5 oz bag of mixed spring greens
2 large Granny Smith apples
48 large white seedless grapes
½ lb. pecorino cheese
1 oz pignolia nuts
4 ½ tbsp olive oil
4 ½ tbsp honey
3 tbsp balsamic vinegar

- Arrange greens on individual salad plates.

- Core and slice apples and place slices over greens.

- Cut grapes in half and sprinkle over greens.

- Crumble pieces of pecorino over salad, and sprinkle with pignolia nuts.

- In a measuring cup, whisk together olive oil, honey, and balsamic vinegar to taste.

- Pour dressing over salad, and serve immediately.

Apple Cake

1/4 pound unsalted butter
1 cup milk
1 cup sugar
4 large eggs
salt
1 lemon
2 cups flour
1 tbsp baking powder
butter spray
2 large golden apples
granulated sugar

- Preheat oven to 350 degrees Fahrenheit.

- In a small pan, heat butter and milk on low to soften. Let cool and set aside.

- Put sugar, eggs, and a pinch of salt in a large mixing bowl.

- Zest the lemon into the bowl and whisk all together.

- Add cooled melted butter and milk to mixture and whisk quickly.

- Whisk in flour. Mixture will look like custard.

- Add baking powder while whisking.

- Spray 10-inch spring form pan with butter spray and pour in mixture.

- Peel, core, and slice apples.

- Arrange apple slices on top in desired design, gently pushing them slightly into custard.

- Place in oven and bake for 50 minutes, or when a toothpick inserted in center comes out clean.

- Remove from oven and sprinkle with granulated sugar while hot and still in pan.

- Remove spring side and serve.

Bibliography of Reference Books Used for the Trip

Baedeker's *Italy*. New York: Random House, 1999.

Bramblett, Reid, and Lynn A. Levine. Frommer's *Italy From $70 A Day*. New York: Wiley, 2003.

Bramblett, Ried. Frommer's *Tuscany & Umbria*. New York: Macmillan, 2002.

Brown, Karen. *Italy: Charming Inns & Itineraries*. San Mateo, California: Karen Brown's Guides, 2004.

Duncan, Paul. Frommer's *Italy's Best-Loved Driving Tours*. New York: Wiley, 2003.

Time Out Naples: Capri, Sorrento & the Amalfi Coast. London: Penguin Books, 2002.

Padua • • Venice

Florence •

San Gimignano •
Siena • Cooking School
• Assisi
Spoleto • Roseto degli Abruzzi
Orvieto • Pacentro
Cocullo • Sulmona
Rome • • Bugnara

Naples •
Sorento • Positano
Capri • • Ravello

Messina • Villa San Giovanni
Mt. Etna △ • Taormina

978-0-595-45423-5
0-595-45423-2

Printed in the United States
200277BV00004B/430-438/A